Sinbad the Sailor

A pantomime

Paul Reakes

W0013840

Samuel French – London
New York – Sydney – Toronto – Hollywood

CHARACTERS

Dame Semolina Sinbad
Grand Vizier
The Sultan of Baghdad
Princess Yasmin
Vazar (an evil magician)
Hassan (his assistant)
Sinbad
Captain (of the *Golden Hawk*)
Mister Mate
Monty (the Monkey)
Barracuda (the Witch of the Sea)
Black Hook (a pirate captain)
Yellow Jack ⎫ Pirates
Blue Peter ⎭
A Camel
Genie of the Magic Ring
Citizens of Baghdad, Guards, Handmaidens, Sailors, Pirates, Belly Dancers, People of Zalabar, Skeleton Dancers, Valley Dwellers.

SYNOPSIS OF SCENES

ACT I
SCENE 1 Old Baghdad
SCENE 2 Above the Valley of Skulls
SCENE 3 Galley of the *Golden Hawk*
SCENE 4 Deck of the *Golden Hawk*

ACT II
SCENE 1 Above the Valley of Skulls
SCENE 2 The Slave Market
SCENE 3 On the way to Black Hook's Tent
SCENE 4 Black Hook's Tent
SCENE 5 Above the Valley of Skulls
SCENE 6 The Valley of Skulls
SCENE 7 Above the Valley of Skulls
SCENE 8 Before the Wedding
SCENE 9 Sinbad's Wedding. Finale

SINBAD THE SAILOR

First presented at the Little Theatre, Wells, Somerset,
with the following cast:

Dame Semolina Sinbad	Alan Taylor
Grand Vizier	Ron Norton
The Sultan of Baghdad	Harry Parkes
Princess Yasmin	Trudie Dowell
Vazar (an evil magician)	Paul Reakes
Hassan (his assistant)	Marcus Carter
Sinbad	Sylvia Butt
Captain (of the *Golden Hawk*)	Chris Lavis
Mister Mate	Ivor Baulch
Monty (the monkey)	Karen Boyd
Barracuda (the Witch of the Sea)	Jenny Veal
Black Hook (a pirate captain)	Peter Taylor
Yellow Jack ⎫ (Pirates)	Nick Crowley
Blue Peter ⎭	Richard Salvidge
A Camel	Jean Johnson
	Pauline Norton
Genie of the Magic Ring	Marcus Carter

MUSIC PLOT

ACT I

1	Song	Chorus
2	Comic Song	Dame
3	Song and Dance	Yasmin, Handmaidens and Chorus
4	Song	Sinbad and Chorus
5	Comic Dance	Monty, Sinbad, Dame, Captain and Mate
6	Duet	Sinbad and Yasmin
7	Song and Dance	Sinbad, Dame, Monty, Captain, Mate and Chorus
8	Song and Dance	Sinbad and Chorus
9	Song	Mate, Captain and Sinbad
10	Song and Dance	Sinbad, Yasmin and Handmaidens
11	Song and Dance	Black Hook and Pirates

ACT II

12	Song	Black Hook, Pirates and Chorus
13	Belly Dance	Belly Dancers
14	Song	Sinbad and Chorus
15	Comic Striptease Dance	Dame
16	Dance	Belly Dancers, Pirates or Camel
17	Song	Sinbad, Dame and Monty
18	Comic Dance	Captain and Mate
19	Dance	Skeleton Dancers
20	Song	Yasmin and Chorus
21	Sing-a-long	Dame, Captain, Mate, Monty, Camel and Audience
22	Finale Song	All

PRODUCTION NOTES

The pantomime offers opportunities for elaborate staging, but can be produced quite simply if facilities are limited. There are five full sets:
Old Baghdad
Deck of the *Golden Hawk*
The Slave Market
The Valley of Skulls
Sinbad's Wedding—Finale
And two half sets:
Galley of the *Golden Hawk*
Black Hook's Tent
All these scenes are interlinked by tabs or frontcloth scenes.

The *Golden Hawk* and pirate ship are well painted cut-outs that are pushed on smoothly from the wings. The Sea Serpent should give the audience a fright, and is well worth some careful thought and clever engineering. It should have movable jaws and eyes that glow. Lighting and sound effects are very important. There are plenty of flashes, weird noises, thunder and lightning, a flying carpet and a giant bird! Carefully controlled ground mist will enhance the dream scene in Act I and the Valley of Skulls' scene in Act II. The dumplings that Monty throws at the audience should be made of a substance weighty enough to be thrown but harmless on impact.

CHARACTERS AND COSTUMES

Dame Sinbad is a lovable old girl who enjoys both fun and misery. Her costumes are all outrageous and comic in Eastern design.

Grand Vizier is a haughty gent in official gown and turban.

The Sultan is master of all he surveys. He is bearded and bedecked in magnificent robes and jewelled turban.

Princess Yasmin is a beautiful young woman with a sweet voice and manner. She shows a different side to her character however when standing up to Vazar. It goes without saying that all her costumes are exquisite.

Vazar is an evil magician, an out-and-out villain. He wears a black turban and black flowing gown decorated with strange, magical symbols. His make-up is sinister Eastern with a black forked beard and curling eyebrows.

Hassan (child's part) is Vazar's downtrodden little assistant. A short, ragged robe and tatty turban.

Sinbad (principal boy) is a dashing young swashbuckler with an engaging manner and the best legs on the high seas! He wears Eastern blouses with colourful sashes and turbans.

The Captain is a hearty old sea salt whose bark is worse than his bite. Apart from his captain's jacket, sea boots and tricorn hat, he gets to wear Arab and comic Belly-Dancer's costumes.

Mister Mate is a lovable nitwit with a gormless expression, a crazy laugh and a watery "lithp". He wears a knee-length striped jersey and a silly little sailor hat. He also gets to appear in Arab and Belly-Dancer's costume.

Monty the Monkey (female or child's part) is a mischievous little chimp, full of comic capers. A good monkey skin with flexible face. He wears a little bolero and fez, a pair of baggy swimming shorts and a chef's hat.

Barracuda is Vazar's aquatic partner in crime. A soggy villainess, with seaweed like hair, scales and webbed fingers.

Black Hook is a big, bloodthirsty pirate, who would sell his own granny for a thimble of grog! He sports a bushy black beard and has a vicious steel hook instead of a right/left hand. He wears the traditional pirate captain's outfit, armed to the teeth with cutlasses and pistols.

The Camel is a two-person comic experience on four legs! A good panto camel skin with movable eyelids and mouth.

The Genie (child's part) is a polite little bit of Arabian magic. The costume and make-up is green with glitter on hands and face.

Yellow Jack and Blue Peter are burly pirates.

The Chorus have lots to do, appearing as Citizens of Baghdad, Sailors, Pirates, Valley Dwellers and Townsfolk.

Children can appear as Street Urchins, Junior Sailors, Pirates and Valley Dwellers. All are involved in the action and musical numbers.

Dancers appear as Handmaidens, Sailors, Pirates, Belly Dancers and the gruesome Skeleton Dancers.

Other titles by Paul Reakes in French's Acting Editions

One Act Plays:
Bang, You're Dead!
Mantrap

Pantomimes:
Little Miss Muffet
Santa in Space a Christmas pantomime adventure

open main curtains

ACT I

SCENE 1

Old Baghdad

Prominent, L, is the Sultan's sumptuous palace. R, are bright stalls piled with carpets, fruit, pots, etc. UC, are steps leading to the harbour wall. The backcloth shows Baghdad harbour

As the CURTAIN rises, Eastern-type music plays and the stage is teeming with the Citizens of Baghdad. All is noise and bustle. Stall-holders cry their wares, and beggars cry for alms. Once the scene is set, the music changes and the Citizens start to sing

1. Song (Chorus)

After the song, Dame Sinbad enters DL, carrying a shopping bag

Dame (*hollering at someone off* L) And you can keep yer rotten old cabbages! I wouldn't buy 'em now, not even if you threw in the caterpillars free! I've got a good mind to report you to Esther Rancid! Sellin' rubbish like that! I'm goin' to shop at (*local shop*) from now on! (*She pokes out her tongue*) So there! (*To the audience*) That's tellin' 'em!

A large cabbage flies out from the wings and hits her. She yells and falls over

The Citizens laugh and exit

(*Getting up and rubbing her rear*) Cor! I bet I've crushed me curly kale! (*Looking at her bag*) No, they're OK. (*Waving*) Hello, folks! Hi, kids! I'm Dame Semolina Sinbad, but you can call me Semolina. Now, let's do it proper. When I shout "hello, folks", I want you all to shout back "Hello, Semolina". Think you can do that?

Audience: "Yes"

Smashin'! Here goes. (*Waving*) Hello, folks!

The audience shout back

Great! You deserve a reward for that. (*She takes sweets from her bag and throws them at the audience*) Here you are! Catch! (*etc.*) (*During the ad libs, she takes out an egg carton, opens it and offers to throw an egg out*) Who'd like one of this sort?

The audience react

No? Why not? (*She sees the egg*) Oh, silly me! That could have been messy! The *yolk* would have been on you then. (*She looks at the egg*) Huh, it's cracked! (*She throws it away and it bounces*) Must be a spring chicken! Well, I can't stand 'ere all day. I've got lots to do. My son Sinbad is comin' 'ome today. He's a sailor, y'know. Oh, I'm ever so excited! In fact, I'm so excited I think I'll give me larynx an airing! (*Archly, to someone in the front row*) That means I feel like singin', you mucky pup! You can all join in with the chorus!

2. Song (Dame Sinbad)

She can have a comic dance during or following the song

(*Making a grand exit* DR *and waving to the audience*) Ta Ta! Bye! See you later!

The Dame trips and staggers out, bow-legged, DR

A gong sounds

The Citizens rush on. Guards enter from the palace, followed by the Grand Vizier

Vizier (*banging his staff*) Make way! Make way! Make way for his Mighty Magnificence, the Sultan of Baghdad!

The gong sounds. The Citizens fall to their knees

To suitable music, the Sultan enters grandly from the palace

Citizens (*bowing*) Salaam! O mighty one. Salaam!
Sultan Good citizens of Baghdad, I have joyful tidings to impart. Today is the eighteenth birthday of my most beauteous daughter!
Citizens (*bowing*) Allah be praised!
Sultan Behold! The Princess Yasmin!   TAFFETA

The gong sounds

To suitable music, lovely Princess Yasmin enters from the palace, followed by Handmaidens

Citizens (*bowing*) Salaam, O Mighty Princess, Salaam!
Yasmin (*aside to the Sultan*) Have you told them yet, Father?
Sultan Nay, my child.
Yasmin Then please let me. It would give me great pleasure.
Sultan If it so pleases thee, O light of my life!
Yasmin Salaam! (*To the Citizens*) Good people, may Allah have mercy on your poor knees. Please rise.

The Citizens stand

As you know, today is my birthday. In celebration, my most generous father has declared it a public holiday for one and all.
Citizens (*overjoyed*) Salaam! Salaam!
Sultan Thou art all free to spend the entire day in total idleness. I have spoken. (*Holding his hand out to Yasmin*) Come, O joy of my declining years.

He and Yasmin move towards the palace. Suddenly, Yasmin remembers something and forgets her regal bearing

Yasmin Hang on a minute, Pop!
Sultan (*aghast*) Daughter! No pleasantry in front of the peasantry!
Yasmin (*suppressing her laughter*) I beg forgiveness. It is just that we have forgotten the custom.
Sultan Custom?
Yasmin It is the ancient custom of Baghdad that a princess should sing in public on her eighteenth birthday.
Sultan Thou art right, O jogger of my memory. So be it! Carry out the custom.

Yasmin bows to him and sings

3. Song (Yasmin, Handmaidens and Chorus)

A dance for Yasmin and Handmaidens can follow the song

After the number, the Sultan and Yasmin exit into the palace, followed by the Vizier, Handmaidens and Guards

The sinister figure of Vazar enters DR

Vazar (*snarling to someone off* R) Make haste, you crawling worm! You sluggard!

Little Hassan staggers on carrying a large black box decorated with magic symbols

Bah! You are slower than a snail with bunions!
Hassan (*gasping*) I—I beg forgiveness, O Mighty Master. This box is so heavy.
Vazar You smell of a thousand drains! One more complaint and I'll turn you into a toad! Then you'll *hop* it! (*Laughing his grisly laugh*) Ha! Ha! Ha! Laugh dog! Your master has made a funny!

Hassan laughs weakly

(*Seeing the palace*) Ah, the sultan's palace! At last my journey is over.

Hassan puts the box down and sits on it, exhausted. Vazar bows to the audience in Eastern fashion

Salaams and greetings, O miserable minions! I am Vazar, Master of Magicians! No doubt you have heard of me? No! Well, I'm a sort of hairy Paul Daniels! Full of Eastern promise. I have come to Baghdad to perform my magic at the princess's birthday party tonight. My visit is very innocent. (*He gives a sinister laugh*) Hee! Hee! Hee! (*To Hassan*) Up, dog! We go to the sultan.

He moves to the palace, pushing the Citizens aside. Hassan picks up the box and totters after him

(*To a beggar*) Out of my way, ragged riff-raff!

He is about to enter the palace as:

The Grand Vizier enters

Vizier Hold!
Vazar Stand aside, minion! I have business with the sultan.
Vizier Who are you?
Vazar Who am *I*? I am Vazar the Mighty, Master of all Magicians!
Vizier Prove it, O Boastful One!
Vazar Very well! You asked for it! (*He waves his hands about and starts to chant*) By the powers of darkness and the curse of witches, may you be plagued by a thousand—*itches*!

He makes a magic pass at the Vizier who starts scratching, uncontrollably

Ha! Ha! Ha! That will teach you to doubt the Powers of Vazar the Mighty! Ha! Ha! Ha!

Laughing, Vazar exits into the palace, followed by Hassan. The Vizier, still scratching like mad, follows

Woman He really *is* a great magician!
1st Man Ay, and a nasty one at that!
2nd Man I hope the sultan knows what he is doing inviting a person like *that* into his palace!

The others agree. A ship's bell is heard off, UR

Sinbad (*off,* UR) Ahoy there! Ahoy!
Citizens It's Sinbad! Sinbad the Sailor! (*They all turn upstage*)

To suitable music, the figure-head and part of the Golden Hawk *appears behind the harbour from* UR

The handsome, young Sinbad the Sailor is standing on deck, waving

Sinbad Ahoy there!
Citizens (*waving back*) Ahoy, Sinbad!

Sinbad jumps from the ship and comes forward. The Citizens greet him warmly

Sinbad (*to the audience*) Ahoy, shipmates! Come on, let's hear you! Ahoy, shipmates!

Audience: "Ahoy, Sinbad!"

Yes, I'm Sinbad. Sinbad the Sailor! I've been away at sea for a whole year, exploring foreign parts. The strangest place we visited was (*neighbouring village or town*)! The natives there are a very odd lot, I can tell you. They only eat toffee and super glue! Oh, they're very stuck up! Ah, dear old Baghdad! Home, sweet home! You know, mateys, I love going to sea, but it's great to come home. (*He sings*)

4. Song (Sinbad and Chorus)

After the song, the Citizens exit

Dame Sinbad enters DR

(*Speaking*) Mum!

Dame Sinny! (*Rushing over and hugging him*) Oh, my Sinny Winny! My little baby boy home from the sea! Let Mummy give you a big kissy-wissy! (*She smothers him with noisy, juicy kisses*)

Sinbad (*laughing*) Steady on, Mum! (*He wipes his face*) I haven't got my life-belt with me!

Dame Let's have a good gander at ya! (*She does so*) Oh, you look grand! This seafarin' certainly seems to suit you, Sinbad! (*Business with her teeth*) Cor! I nearly lost me top set! (*To the audience*) Well, what do you think of my boy? Isn't he a humdinger? I bet you wish you had a son like that. (*To someone in the front row*) What d'you mean, you'd be worried if you had a son like that! He takes after his father. *He* had good legs as well. They were so good they ran out on me twenty years ago, and never came back!

Sinbad And how have you been keeping, Mum?

Dame (*hand to forehead, very tragic*) Oh, don't ask me! *Don't* ask me!

Sinbad (*smiling and moving away*) OK!

Dame (*pulling him back*) Come 'ere! Oh, it's been one catastrophe after another! Your Uncle Abdul and Aunt Salome had a gas explosion. They got blown clean through the window! Yes! It's the first time they've been out together for years! And then Cousin Fatima's 'usband ran off and left 'er without a penny! She's so hard up, she has to put both her babies in *one* nappy! It's the only way she can make both ends meet! And I've 'ad me old trouble again! It starts in me diagram and shoots right down to me shinguards!

Sinbad (*putting his arm around her*) Never mind, Mum, *I'm* home now!

Dame (*hugging him*) That you are, Sinny! And you couldn't have picked a better day to come home. It's Princess Yasmin's birthday and the old sultana has declared it a public 'oliday. We must celebrate! We'll go down to the *Eunuch's Arms* and 'ave a couple of highballs!

Sinbad I've brought you back a present.

Dame Oh, goody-goody gumdrops! What is it?

Sinbad What do you need more than anything else in the world?

Dame (*to the audience*) Don't any of you dare answer that! (*To Sinbad*) Is it a new set of choppers?

Sinbad No. It's something to keep you company while I'm away at sea. Now, shut your eyes and I'll go and fetch it.

Very excited, the Dame shuts her eyes tightly

During the following, Sinbad runs to the ship and exits. He re-enters immediately, followed by the Captain and Mate who carry a large Ali-Baba basket between them. The Mate has a toy parrot on his shoulder. They place the basket downstage. The Mate stands near it, a gormless, zombie-like expression on his face

Dame Oh, I can't wait to see what it is! Hurry up, Sinny! Come on, or me eyes'll go to sleep! I'm in a very venerable position 'ere, y'know! Hurry up! 'Ave ya gone to (*far away place*) to get it?

Sinbad You can open your eyes now, Mum.

She does so and finds the Captain standing beside her

Dame (*thrilled*) Ooo! Sinny! You *are* a good boy! He's just what the doctor ordered. Me own Popeye the Sailorman! (*Fluttering her eyelashes at the Captain*) Hello, sailor!

Captain Avast behind!

Dame 'Ere, there's no need to get personal!

Sinbad (*pulling her away*) Mum! That's my Captain. The Captain of the *Golden Hawk*.

Dame (*to the audience*) Looks more like the Captain of (*local football team*) to me!

Captain Why, shiver me timbers an' rumple me riggin'! So you be young Sinbad's ma, eh? Crumple me capstan an' pickle me poopdeck! I be right pleased to meet 'ee! Ha har!

Dame (*copying him*) Ha har! Why, buckle me brooms an' dent me dustpan! I be right pleased to meet *'ee*, Cap'n! Oh, ar! Jim lad! Ha har!

She hops about on one leg, à la Long John Silver. The Captain roars with laughter and slaps her on the back. She falls flat on the floor

Sinbad (*helping her up*) Come and see your present, Mum.

He leads the Dame to the basket. She sees the zombie-like Mate standing there and does a huge double-take

Dame (*aside to Sinbad*) What's *that*?

Sinbad He's one of the crew. He's the first mate.

Dame Yeah! He looks as if he's been around a long time.

She peers at the Mate who just stares into space

(*To someone in the audience*) Is 'e with you?

Sinbad (*pointing to the basket*) Here's your present.

Dame Huh! Some present! An old basket for an old basket! (*With an indignant toss of the head*) Ta very much, I *don't* think!

Captain The present be inside, you silly landlubber!

Dame Oo! Captain! Wash your mouth out! (*To Sinbad, excited again*) Open it up! Open it up!

Sinbad Close your eyes first.

Dame Oh, what *again*!

Captain (*roaring*) Ar!

Dame (*jumping with fright*) Ahh! Oh, anything you say, Captain Birdseye! (*She shuts her eyes, then opens them again; wagging a finger at the Captain*) Now, don't you go taking advantage of me. I've heard all about you naughty sailor boys!

Captain Batten down yer 'atch and shut yer port'oles!

Dame (*to the audience*) Oh, he's *so* masterful! (*She shuts her eyes*) Ready!

Sinbad opens the basket. The head of a little monkey appears over the top. It climbs out of the basket and Sinbad leads it over to the Dame. The monkey looks at her, scratches its head, then proceeds to tickle the Dame under the chin

(*Squirming with delight*) Ooo! Captain! You *naughty* man! I'm not that sort of girl! Oh! Give over! *Stop it!*

The monkey stops its antics and Dame grunts with disappointment

Huh! There's no need to take me liberally!

Sinbad Open your eyes, Mum.

She does so and comes face to face with the monkey. She yells and hides behind the Captain

Mum, this is Monty the Monkey.

Dame (*peeping out from behind the Captain*) No, it's not! Why didn't you tell me you'd found yer father!

Sinbad Come and say hello to Monty.

Dame No flippin' fear!

Captain (*pulling her out from behind him*) Don't 'ee be afeared, Mother Sinbad. 'E be quite tame. We brought 'im all the way back from an unexplored part o' the world.

Dame What—(*local place*)? Well, you can take 'im right back there!

Monty (*holding out his paw to the Dame*) Oo! Oo! Oo!

Dame (*jumping back into the Captain's arms*) Ahh! What's it tryin' to do to me!?

Sinbad He only wants to shake hands with you. Don't you, Monty?

Monty (*nodding*) Oo! (*He holds out his paw to the Dame*)

Dame Well, I . . . (*To the Captain*) Shall I?

Captain Ar!

Dame (*to the audience*) Do you think I should?

Audience: "Yes"

All right! I'll chance it.

She timidly takes Monty's paw and they shake. The Dame warms to Monty and goes "Ahh" to the audience

Sinbad Now then, Monty, you show Mum what else you can do.

Dame No thanks! I *know* what else 'e can do! I've been to the Zoo!

Sinbad (*to Monty*) Show her how you can dance. Go on, Monty—dance!

5. Dance (Monty, Dame, Sinbad, Captain, Mate)

This should be a comic dance started by Monty and then involving the others. The Mate dances alone, still with gormless expression

Monty (*rubbing his belly*) Oo! Oo! Oo!

Dame What's 'e doin' now! Dare I ask!

Sinbad That means he's hungry.

Monty (*nodding*) Oo! Oo!

Sinbad (*taking his paw*) Right! Let's take you home and find you something to eat.

Dame 'Ere! Just a minute! I'm not 'avin' monkeys eatin' in *my* house!

Sinbad That's all right, Mum, Monty's not particular!

Sinbad exits R *with Monty, who waves to the audience as he goes out*

Dame What a flippin' cheek! (*Moving to the Captain and fluttering her eyelashes*) What about you, Captain? Do you fancy a little nibble?

Captain Ar!

Dame Come on then, let's see what I can tempt you with. (*She leads him upstage, then spots the Mate*) I suppose I'd better ask chatterbox! (*She moves close to Mate; loudly and slowly*) Would—you—like—something—to—eat?

Mate (*suddenly coming alive with a watery "lithp"*) Yeth pleath!

Dame (*reeling back and wiping her eye*) Well, *say* it, don't *spray* it! (*Pointing to the parrot*) What about Buzby? Would he like something? How about some—— (*to the audience*)—wait for it! (*To the Mate*) How about some Pollyfiller!

She falls about laughing. The Mate remains deadpan

Mate (*pointing to the parrot*) He'th thick.

Dame *He's* not the only one!

Mate I'd give him thome athpirinth, but we ain't got none left.

Dame Why not?

Mate Coth, the-parroth-eat-'em-all. (*Paracetamol*) Ha! Ha! Ha! Ha! (*He gives a wild, crazy laugh that goes on for quite a while. Suddenly it stops dead, and he returns to gormless deadpan*)

Dame (*to the Captain*) You know, we could do with 'im out *there*! (*She points to the audience*) Come on, let's get some nosh!

She leads the Captain out R. *The Mate follows with the basket. Just before he exits, he gives the audience another burst of his crazy laughter*

Princess Yasmin enters from the palace. She moves downstage, deep in thought. The Handmaidens run from the palace and gather around her

1st Handmaiden Princess! You should not be out of the palace on your own.

2nd Handmaiden Your father would be most displeased.

3rd Handmaiden Is something troubling you, O Mighty One?

Yasmin (*with a deep sigh*) Oh, dear! I should be the happiest girl in the whole world. I live in a sumptuous palace. I want for nothing. I have charm, wit, grace, intelligence and great beauty. And above all, Allah has seen fit to bless me with a modest disposition. But, I feel that something is missing from my life. Something that ... oh, I cannot explain! (*A deep sigh*)

The girls giggle behind their hands

Why do you laugh?

They giggle

(*In a huff*) Be gone from my sight!

1st Handmaiden But your Highness——
Yasmin Be gone, I say! (*She claps her hands*)

Giggling, the girls run into the palace

Yasmin turns away in annoyance

Sinbad enters UR. *He sees her and comes down, gazing adoringly*

Sinbad (*to the audience*) Cor! What a smasher! She must be Princess Yasmin.

Yasmin turns and sees Sinbad. He drops down on one knee and bows

Sinbad Salaam, O Mighty Princess. May a humble commoner be permitted to wish you a happy birthday?
Yasmin (*with icy dignity*) You may. (*Melting a little*) Who are you?
Sinbad I am Sinbad. Sinbad the Sailor!
Yasmin Please rise.

He stands and moves DR. *Yasmin moves* DL. *They face front*

Yasmin (*to the audience*) He has lovely manners for a common sailor. And he is so handsome. I must confess, he gives me a strange feeling here! (*She touches her heart*) Could it be that *he* is the something missing from my life?
Sinbad (*to the audience*) What do you think of her, shipmates? She's a right little cracker, isn't she? Shiver me timbers, if I'm not head over heels in love with her!
Yasmin⎫ (*together, turning to each other*) ⎰Sinbad ...
Sinbad ⎭ ⎱Princess ...
Yasmin (*laughing, taking a step nearer*) After you.
Sinbad (*doing the same*) No, Princess, after *you*.
Yasmin Is it true what they say about sailors?
Sinbad Is *what* true?
Yasmin (*a step nearer*) That they have a different girl in every port?
Sinbad (*a step nearer*) Well, it's not true in my case.
Yasmin (*delighted*) Oh, I'm so glad ... I mean ... (*A step back; shyly*) I—I see.
Sinbad (*a step nearer*) Up until now my ship and my old mum have been the only girls in my life.
Yasmin (*a step nearer*) Up until now? What do you mean?
Sinbad I think you know. (*He sings*)

6. Song (Sinbad and Yasmin)

A romantic duet with romantic lighting

Yasmin Oh, Sinbad! Do you really love me?
Sinbad With all my heart! Let's get my captain to marry us at once!
Yasmin (*with a sigh*) If only we could. (*She moves away*) But it's impossible.
Sinbad Why?

Yasmin I am the daughter of a sultan and you are but a common sailor.

Sinbad (*to the audience*) I love her dearly, but she's a bit of a snob. (*To Yasmin*) In matters of love all are equal.

Yasmin Very true, but I doubt if my father will see it that way.

Sinbad (*taking her in his arms*) Then what is to be done, my beloved?

Yasmin (*in tears*) I don't know!

Sinbad Oh, Yasmin!

Yasmin Oh, Sinbad!

The Dame enters DR *quickly*

Dame (*seeing them*) Oh, heck!

Yasmin breaks from Sinbad and runs crying into the palace

The Dame grabs Sinbad's hand and smacks it

Sinbad! You naughty, naughty boy! You can't go canoodlin' with the royal icing like that! Her dad'll 'ave you decaffeinated on the spot!

Sinbad (*over the moon*) Oh, Mum! The princess and I love each other!

Dame Don't talk so wet! She doesn't love you! *You*, a tatty tar without testimonials! Yer off yer chump, you chump!

Sinbad (*spinning her around*) I'm in love! I'm in love! I'm in love!

Dame (*dizzy*) Steady! Steady! (*Suddenly struck*) 'Ere! You really mean it, don't ya? You *are* in love.

Sinbad Yes, and it's absolutely marvellous!

Dame (*sniffing*) Yes ... it's—it's ... marvellous! (*Burying her face in her apron and crying*) Boo hoo!

Sinbad Don't cry, Mum. You're supposed to be happy for me.

Dame (*wailing*) I am! I am! Oh! My little baby boy in love! (*To the audience*) It only seems like yesterday I was washin' his little *this* and powderin' his little *that*! (*To Sinbad*) I suppose this means you'll be gettin' hitched and leavin' yer poor old mummy!

Sinbad (*sadly*) No such luck! The sultan would never consent to his daughter marrying a commoner.

Dame (*very indignant*) What! Is he incineratin' your family's rubbish!

Sinbad There's only one way he'll let me marry Yasmin. I must become rich and famous!

Dame What like that lot up (*local posh area*)?

Sinbad I said famous, not *infamous*.

Dame But how are you going to do it, Sinny?

Sinbad I don't know yet. But I'll find a way, Mum! I'll find a way!

Sinbad marches out DL

Dame (*calling after him*) That's ma boy! (*To the audience*) I hope he does find a way, don't you, kids? It'll be nice havin' a royal princess in the family. (*Putting on an ultra-posh voice and manner*) I shall have caviar and chips for breakfast, before I take the corgies for their walkies. (*She sticks her nose in the air and walks majestically to exit* DR. *She gives the audience a royal wave*) Olive oil, peasants! (*She trips near the exit, ruining the whole*

Open Fatma song Daisy bring on ecca matts 11

effect) Stone the crows! (*Looking at the ground*) There ought be a law against them flippin' camels! *close blue certains*

The Dame flounces out

To suitable chase music, Monty scampers on UL, *pursued by an exhausted Mate. They do a lap of the stage and the Mate falls to the ground, shattered. Monty runs out* DR. *The Captain runs on* UL

Captain Monty! Monty! Where be that monkey? By thunder, Mister Mate, you've let 'im get away! Which way did 'e go?

The Mate lifts an arm weakly then falls back

(*To the audience*) Ahoy, me hearties! Did any of 'ee see where the monkey went?

Audience: "Out there!" "That way." Etc.

(*Roaring off* DR) Monty! This be your captain shoutin'! Come 'ere at once! (*Nothing*) There be only one thing for it. Mister Mate!
Mate (*staggering to his feet*) Yeth, Cap'n?
Captain You'll 'ave to give the special monkey call.
Mate (*shyly*) I feel thilly, Cap'n.
Captain Belay! Give the call! That be an order!
Mate (*to the audience*) Oh, thith ith tho embarrathin! (*Beating his chest and making monkey noises*) Oo! Oo! Oo!
Captain By thunder! That bain't loud enough! Louder! Louder!
Mate I can't "Oo, Oo" any louder, Cap'n. Why don't you ath the nith ladieth an' gentlemen, an' boyth and girlth to help.
Captain Ar! (*To the audience*) Will 'ee help, shipmates? All you 'ave to do is beat yer chests an' make monkey noises. That'll be easy for some of 'ee! After three then. One! Two! Three!

He, the Mate and the audience perform. Ad lib and comic business as the captain gets the audience to do it again

Monty creeps back upstage

(*To the audience*) Any sign o' that monkey yet?

Audience: "He's behind you!" Comic business with them turning and Monty keeping behind them. "Oh, no he isn't! Oh, yes he is!" routine. Eventually they discover Monty standing between them. They take big steps backwards and prepare to rush him. As they charge, Monty steps back and they crash into each other and fall over

Monty, chattering with laughter, skips out DL, *waving to the audience as he goes*

The gong sounds

Sinbad and the Citizens rush on

What's all the excitement, Sinbad? Somebody won the Pools? (*Or local gag*)

Sinbad The Sultan is coming!

The gong sounds

> *Guards enter from the palace, followed by the Grand Vizier*

Vizier (*banging his staff*) Make way! Make way for His Mighty Magnificence—the Sultan of Baghdad! Make way for *Her* Mighty Magnificence—the Princess Yasmin!

The gong sounds. All fall to their knees. Comic business with Captain and the Mate

> *The Sultan and Yasmin enter, followed by Handmaidens*

All (*bowing*) Salaam! O mighty ones! Salaam!
Sultan Good people of Baghdad, rise!

All stand

> *Dame Sinbad runs on* DR *and throws herself at the Sultan's feet*

Dame (*bowing*) O Salami! O Polony! May your bath-tub never run over! May your toilet-roll never run out! (*She hauls herself up by the Sultan's robes*) Sorry I'm late, yer Royal Raisin. I had to feed the Camel or he'll get the hump! (*She guffaws and nudges the Sultan*) Get it? Camel—hump? Oh, please yerself!
Sinbad (*trying to pull her away*) Mum!
Dame (*pushing him away*) Don't be so rude! Can't you see I'm chattin' to his effluence the sultana. (*To the Sultan*) I'm Mrs Sinbad, but as we'll soon be family, you can call me Semolina.
Sultan What dost thou mean, woman?
Dame Never mind the dustin' ... (*Nudging him*) You know! When my Sinbad and your——
Vizier (*behind the Dame*) Silence! His Magnificence is about to speak!
Dame All right, Lord Snooty! Don't get yer turban in a tangle! (*To the Sultan*) Go ahead, your Sultanship.
Sultan (*to everyone*) Tonight, in honour of my daughter's birthday, a great feast will be held in the royal palace.
Dame Oo! A posh nosh! (*To the Sultan*) Well, go on! Go on!
Sultan After the feasting there will be a special entertainment. An entertainment the like of which has never been seen in Baghdad before!
Dame Don't say you've got the (*local society*)!
All (*to the Dame*) Ssh!
Sultan At enormous expense I have procured the services of the world's greatest magician. Vazar, the Mighty!

There is a flash

> *Vazar appears* DL

All react

Dame Crikey! It's Dirty Bertie from Number Thirty!

> *Hassan follows Vazar on, carrying the box*

Vazar (*taking* C) I am Vazar, Master of all Magicians! My mighty magical marvels mystify many millions!

Dame (*impressed*) Cor! That was good! Can you say—Peter Piper picked a——

Vazar (*snubbing her; turning to Sultan*) Your Magnificence! O Ruler of Rulers! (*He bows. To Yasmin*) Your Highness! O Beauty of Beauties! (*He bows*)

Dame Ger off! O Creep of Creeps!

Vazar (*snarling at her*) Silence, hag!

Dame 'Ere, *Mrs* Hag, to you!

Vazar (*to the Sultan*) O mighty one, may I be permitted to demonstrate a little of my magic now? Just as a taste of what wonders I have in store for you tonight.

Sultan So be it.

Vazar bows and prepares for magic by putting his hands to his head and groaning deeply

Dame (*to the audience*) Is there a packet of Rennies in the house?

Vazar (*chanting*)   Abracadabra! Abracadee!
                          Magical powers come to me!
                          Abracadabra! Abracazune——

Dame He's got a face like a shrivelled up prune!

The Citizens roar with laughter, much to the annoyance of Vazar

Vazar (*to the Dame*) How dare you interfere with my incantations!

Dame (*shocked*) I never laid a finger on 'em!

Vazar Be silent! (*His hands to his head*) I am calling up the spirits!

Dame Mine's a large port an' brandy!

Vazar (*snarling at her*) Ahhggrr!

Dame (*wagging her finger at him*) Temper! Temper!

Vazar (*casting a spell on her*)
                          May your feet develop a will of their own!
                          And carry you off, you interfering crone!

He makes magic passes at the Dame's feet. She yelps, jumps in the air, and starts involuntarily running on the spot

Dame *Help!* He's tampered with me tootsies!!

Yelling, the Dame runs out DR

Vazar Bring forth the magic carpet! (*He claps his hands*)

Hassan opens the box and lifts out a roll of exotic carpet. He brings it and unrolls it

(*With a great flourish*) Behold! The magic carpet! (*He steps on to the carpet*) I will now give a demonstration of its amazing powers! (*He holds out his hand to Yasmin*) Come, Princess.

Yasmin May I, Father?

Sultan If it so pleases thee, my child. (*To Vazar*) If thou art sure there is no danger.

Vazar None! (*He holds out his hand*) Come.

Yasmin takes his hand and steps on to the carpet

Yasmin What do I have to do?
Vazar Nothing. I will attend to everything. (*Chanting*)
　　　　　　　　Abracadabra! Abracaday!
　　　　　　　　Up magic carpet, and fly away!

The stage grows suddenly dark and eerie. Vazar seizes Yasmin by the wrist

　　　　　　　Take us both to my secret domain!
　　　　　　　The princess will never see Baghdad again!
　　　　　　　Up and away! Ha! Ha! Ha!

*There is a blinding flash, followed by a Black-out. Weird noises fill the air.
Screams and general uproar*

　　Vazar and Yasmin exit. The carpet is struck

The Lights return to normal

　　Hassan, in terror, runs out DL, pursued by the Vizier and Guards

Captain (*rushing forward, pointing out front*) Bust me bobstays! *Look!*

All look

Sinbad He's flying off with the princess! Oh, no! They've gone! Disappeared
over the mountains!
Sultan (*wailing*) O Allah! O Allah! What am I going to do! My child! My
only child!

　　The Vizier enters DL, followed by Guards who are dragging Hassan

Vizier O mighty one! We have caught the magician's assistant trying to
escape!

*The Guards throw Hassan at the Sultan's feet and stand over him with drawn
swords*

Hassan Mercy! Mercy!
Sultan Silence, dog! Where has he taken my daughter?
Hassan He would kill me if I told you!
Sultan And I will kill you if you don't!

The Guards put their swords to Hassan's throat

Hassan (*gulping*) He—he has taken her to his secret domain. The Valley of
the Skulls on the Island of Zalabar! That is all I know, I swear it!

　　The Guards haul Hassan to his feet and take him into the palace

Sinbad The Island of Zalabar? I've never heard of it.
Captain I 'ave! 'Tis many leagues from 'ere. A mighty difficult place to find.
Sultan (*to the Vizier*) Order my ships to put to sea at once!
Sinbad Wait, your Majesty! Please let me go to Zalabar and rescue the
princess.

Sultan You! Who art thou?
Sinbad (*saluting proudly*) Sinbad the Sailor.
Sultan Hast thou a ship?
Sinbad No—but my captain has!
Captain Thas right . . . (*he gulps*) eh!?
Sinbad And he'll find Zalabar if anyone can. He's the finest navigator on the seven seas!
Captain I'd love to 'elp, but . . .
Sinbad Not scared are you, Cap'n?
Captain (*bracing up*) Scared! Me? Never! (*To the Sultan*) The *Golden Hawk* be at your service! (*He salutes*)
Sultan Nay! 'Twould be folly. One lone ship against the magician's evil power.
Sinbad That's the whole idea. He will be expecting you to send a fleet of ships and have something nasty in store for them. He'll not be suspicious of one small trader. Please, let us try, your Majesty.
Sultan So be it. Thou art a brave lad, Sinbad. If thou returnest my daughter safe, anything thou asketh for will be given unto thee. Captain, prepare thy ship and sail for Zalabar without delay. I have spoken!

The Sultan exits into the palace followed by the Vizier, Handmaidens and Guards. A Guard removes the magic box. The Citizens exit

Captain By thunder! I must 'ave barnacles on the brain lettin' you talk me into this, Sinbad.
Sinbad I must save Yasmin. We love each other. (*A deep sigh*)

The Mate puts his head on Sinbad's shoulder and sighs

Captain Avast there, Mister Mate! Let's get the old ship ready to sail.

The Captain and Mate board the ship and exit. Dame Sinbad enters from
DR

Dame Hey, Sinny! I've just 'eard the news! That nasty old magician's swiped the princess and carted her off on his flyin' Axminster!
Sinbad Don't worry, Mum, I'll soon get her back.
Dame Oh, that's good, I . . . (*Double-take*) Wot you mean? *You'll* soon get 'er back?
Sinbad I'm going to rescue her. The *Golden Hawk* sails at any moment.
Dame I'll come with ya!
Sinbad You can't. Captain never allows women on board!

Sinbad runs to the ship and exits

Dame (*calling after him*) But I'm not a woman! I'm yer mother! (*To the audience*) Oh, dear! What am I goin' to do, boys and girls? I can't let my little boy go on his own! (*Firmly*) I'm goin' with him! I'll get on that ship somehow! But how? How?

The Captain appears on the ship

Captain (*shouting back orders*) Make ready there! Jump to it!

Dame (*to the audience with a wink*) *I* know how! Watch the Joan Collins of
  Baghdad go into action!

*She takes a handkerchief from her knicker leg. The Captain leaves the ship
and, as he moves down, she drops the handkerchief in his path. He picks it up*

Captain Thank'ee. Just wot I need! (*He blows his nose noisily into the hanky*)
Dame (*to the audience*) Well, I'll be blowed!

The Mate and Sinbad enter from the ship and move downstage

Captain Be everything ready, lads?
Mate Yeth, Cap'n. We're ready to thet thail, but I've got thome bad newth.
  The cookth run out on uth. He'th gone to work for (*local fish and chip
  shop or take-away*).
Captain Blisterin' barnacles! We can't sail wi'out a ship's cook! We'd better
  find one fast!

They make for the exit

Dame (*rushing over*) 'Ere! Did I hear you say you needed a cook?
Captain Ar!
Dame What about me? They don't call me the Delia Smith of Baghdad for
  nothing, ya know.
Captain I find that a bit 'ard to swallow!
Dame (*to the audience*) Ha! Wait till he tries the cookin'!
Captain All right, Mother Sinbad, consider yourself engaged.
Dame Oo! I din't know you cared!
Captain As ship's cook!
Dame Oh, goody! That means I can be with you, Sinny. I'll just go and pack
  me portmanteau!
Captain Look lively! I be wantin' to catch the tide!
Dame I always use Persil meself! (*She guffaws at her joke*)

  Dame Sinbad exits DR

The gong sounds

  *The Citizens run on. The Guards enter from the palace, followed by the
  Sultan, Vizier and Handmaidens*

Sultan Captain, art thou ready to sail?
Captain We art, your Majesty!
Sultan Then may Allah protect thee and all those aboard thy ship. May he
  grant that thou findest my daughter and return her safe to me. Allah be
  praised!
All Allah be praised!
Dame (*off*, DR) Go back!

  *The Dame enters, wearing an outrageous coat and hat, and carrying a
  suitcase, hat-box and bird-cage. Monty is following her*

  (*To Monty*) Go back home, you hairy hooligan!
Sinbad What's the matter, Mum?

Dame It's David Bellamy 'ere! He keeps followin' me! (*To Monty*) I'm goin'
to sea, an' you can't come!

Monty turns away, downcast

Sinbad Oh, we can take Monty along, can't we, Cap'n?

Captain Ar! We might as well 'ave two (*indicating the Dame*) monkeys on
board!

Sinbad (*to the audience*) Well, shipmates, here I go! Off to rescue my
beautiful princess. Wish me luck, everyone!

Change clothes
7. Song (Sinbad and Company) *Wish me luck.*

*To end the number, Sinbad, Dame, Monty, Captain and Mate board the ship.
All the others turn upstage to cheer and wave them on their way. The ship
appears to sail off as the Lights fade to Black-out*

blue certins closed

SCENE 2

Above the Valley of Skulls on Zalabar

Tabs, or frontcloth showing mysterious rocks and cliffs. Eerie lighting

Vazar enters R, dragging Princess Yasmin

Vazar Ha! Ha! Ha! Well, here we are, my beautiful one! (*He releases her*)
Welcome to the Island of Zalabar!

Yasmin How dare you bring me here! I am a royal princess. I will not be
treated in this manner! Return me to Baghdad at once!

Vazar Never! You will remain here and become—my bride!

Yasmin Your bride! O Allah protect me! You will pay dearly for this. My
father will rescue me and have you beheaded!

Vazar Ha! Ha! Ha! He may find this island but he will never find *you*!
Come, I have something to show you. (*He drags her to the front of the
stage and points down*) Look down there! *Look, I say!*

She looks and recoils in horror

This is the Valley of Skulls! My secret domain! Once down there, you will
never escape. Only by my magic power can anyone enter or leave the
valley. It will be your home from now on. A perfect cage for such a
beautiful bird!

Yasmin Viper! You cannot imprison me in that foul place!

Vazar I can and I will! Prepare to enter the Valley of Skulls!

Yasmin No! (*She runs L*)

Vazar (*making a magic pass at her*) Kazoom!

*There is a flash and Yasmin is frozen in flight. The general lighting dims and
Vazar and Yasmin are picked out in spotlights. Sinister music*

(*Chanting*)   O Powers of Darkness!
                               O Powers of the Air!

> Transport the fair princess,
> To my secret lair!

There is a flash and the spotlight on Yasmin goes out

> *Yasmin exits*

The Lights return to normal

> (*To the audience, pointing down*) Ha! Ha! Ha! There she is! A tiny speck at the bottom of the valley. She is mine, all mine! Oh, yes, she is. There is no-one who can take her away from me, is there?

Audience: "Yes"

> What! Who?

Audience: "Sinbad"

> Sinbad? What is he?

Audience: "A sailor"

> Is he on his way now?

Audience: "Yes"

> Curse upon curse! Then I must stop him! I know! I will ask my old friend Barracuda, Witch of the Sea, to help me.

The general lighting dims and, to sinister music, a spotlight comes up on Vazar

> From the depths of the ocean, from the slimy sea bed,
> Arise, Barracuda, O Witch most dread!
> O Creature of Seaweed, O Creature of Kelp,
> I command thee come hither, I am in need of thy help!

A blinding flash

> *Barracuda appears* R, *in an eerie green spotlight*

Barracuda (*to the audience*)
> Barracuda the Witch is here!
> I'm the one all sailor boys fear!
> I'll sink any ship, no matter how large,
> And drown all the crew for no extra charge!
> All the monsters that dwell in the deep,
> Do my bidding without giving a peep!
> So, be kind to your goldfish and give him no bover,
> 'Cause he might turn out to be my little bruvver!
> (*To Vazar*)
> I've answered your call from my seabed of slime,
> What's the problem, me old partner in crime?
> But, holy mackerel, you look a bit paler ...

Vazar There's a reason for that! Ever heard of Sinbad the Sailor?

Barracuda   Indeed I have, me evil old mate,
                       He's a goody-goody, the sort that I hate!
Vazar   For reasons which I'll later disclose,
                       That sailor boy gets up my nose!
                       He's on my trail every day,
                       And I want him stopped without delay!
                       Seek out his ship this very morning,
                       And give the brat a dreadful warning!
Barracuda   Say no more! The job is done!
                       To frighten him off will be great fun!
Vazar   Away you go then! Do not linger!
                       Scare him off, me old fish finger!
Barracuda (*to the audience*)
                       Sinbad the Sailor will turn and flee,
                       On seeing Barracuda, the Witch of the Sea!
                       Hee! Hee! Hee!

   A flash and Barracuda has gone

Vazar (*to the audience, gloating*) What do you say now, rabble? She'll soon
scare Sinbad off! He'll go running back to Baghdad with his tail between
his legs! Oh, yes, he will!

Audience reaction

   And when she's finished with him, I'll send her round to see you—on bath
   night! Ha! Ha! Ha!

   Amid boos and hisses, he exits L   ~~blue curtin open~~

The Lights fade to Black-out

SCENE 3

The galley of the Golden Hawk

*The backcloth shows a small galley/cabin with a comic jumble of pots and
pans, a patched hammock, a line of Dame's washing, a broken-down stove with
dirty saucepans, etc. The wings represent masts and rigging and can be used in
the next scene. A table is set* C, *with a rolling pin, cookery book, cooking
utensils, and a bowl of uncooked "dumplings"*

To hornpipe music, Monty dances on L. *He wears a small chef's hat. He capers
about then spots the dumplings. He takes one and starts to nibble it*

Dame (*singing, off* R) "All the nice girls love a sailor . . ." (*etc.*)

   Monty grabs the bowl and scampers off L, *as Dame skips on* R. *She wears a comical sea-cook's outfit with an enormous chef's hat and apron decorated with anchors*

(*Waving to the audience*) Ahoy there, me hearties! Well, here we are, all at sea! Can't say I'm enjoyin' it much! All that wet green stuff goin' up an' down—up an' down! I haven't got a flippin' clue where we are! I got some grit in my eye this mornin' and that's the first bit of land I've seen for days! Well, I can't stand 'ere yappin'. I've got to get the crew's lunch ready. I'm givin' 'em seaweed stew an' dumplings! (*Going to the table*) I've made some smashin' dumplings, I ... Hey! Where's me dumplings?! (*She searches. To the audience*) Whose laid 'ands on my dumplings? Who's had 'em? Was it that monkey?

Audience: "Yes"

I might 'ave known! You wait till I get my 'ands on 'im! (*She gets the rolling pin*) Now, listen kids, if you see him, give me a shout. Shout Mrs Sinbad as loud as you can. Will you do that? Good! (*She strides out* DR, *brandishing the rolling pin*) Come 'ere, you cheeky chimp!

The Dame exits

Monty enters L, *with a bowl*

Audience: "Mrs Sinbad"

Monty runs out R, *as the Dame runs on* L

Where is he? Which way did he go? This way? Right! Don't forget to shout, kids!

She runs out R, *as Monty creeps on* L

The audience shouts

Monty runs out R, *as the Dame runs on* L

Now, I've got 'im, I ... *He's not 'ere!* Which way? Out here? You'd better be right!

She runs out R. *Monty enters* L

The audience shouts. Monty hides under the table

The Dame runs on L. *During the following, Monty creeps out from under the table and scampers off* R

Oh, you lot are 'opeless! You're just messin' me about! It's not fair. Oh, where is he? Where is he?!

Audience: "He's under the table!"

Oh, no he's not!

Audience: "Oh, yes he is!"

Well, I don't believe you! You're 'avin' me on again! Oh, yes, you are! All right! I'll give you all one last chance. I'm goin' to look under the table! (*She looks*) Oo! You little fibbers!

She flounces out R. Monty creeps on backwards from L

The audience shouts

  The Dame creeps on backwards from R

They nearly touch, then circle each other

  (*Facing front; in a loud whisper*) Where is he?

Audience: "Behind you". She turns slowly and so does Monty

  He's not! Where is he now?

Audience: "Behind you". Both turn and this time come face to face. Monty has the bowl hidden behind his back

  Got ya! Where's my dumplings? Have you got 'em?
Monty (*shaking his head*) Oo!
Dame What's behind your back? Hold yer perishin' paws out!

He holds out one paw

  And the *other* one!

Monty whips his paw back and holds the other one out

  Both at the *same* time! (*To the audience*) That's got 'im!

Monty hands her the bowl which she takes without realizing it. He then holds out both paws

  Well! I'll go to the foot of our camel's hump! He hasn't got 'em!

Monty starts to sneak away

  They were in a bowl just like this one, and ... (*Double-take*) *Me dumplings!* (*She grabs Monty*) You 'ad 'em all the time, you bad baboon! (*She takes out a dumpling*) Ugh! Look! He's nibbled one! You mucky monkey! I can't serve these to the crew now! I'll have to throw 'em away!
Monty (*pointing to himself*) Oo! Oo!
Dame Oh, *you* want to throw them away?

Monty nods

  Well, mind that you do it properly. (*She gives him the bowl*) I'll have to make some more. Where's that cookery book? (*She goes to the table and keeps her back to the audience*)

Monty starts to throw the dumplings at the audience. He throws one at the Dame and indicates that the audience should do the same, and they do. Comic business with the Dame and the audience

  The Dame and Monty exit R

  Captain and Mate enter L

Captain Why, can me cod an' tin me tuna! Look at the state o' this galley! That Mother Sinbad is useless!
Mate Yeth, an' theeth bin thayin' thome nathty things about you, Cap'n.

Captain What sort o' things?

Mate Thee thaid you didn't have the brainth of a donkey.

Captain *What!!*

Mate But I thtuck up for you, Cap'n.

Captain Thank'ee, Mister Mate.

Mate I told her you did!

Captain Well done . . . *What!* Why, you scurvy swab! I'll give you a taste o'
the cat!

Mate (*pleased*) Oh! Can I have thome chipth with it?

The Dame enters R

Dame Hello Captain, me old cockle! (*Sidling up to him*) Tell me, have you
come to inspect me quarters? (*Spotting the Mate*) Oh-oh! I see you've got
Sea Spray Sid with you! Oh, Captain, can't we be alone! Take me to some
desert island where we can have a *date* behind the *palms*!

Captain Belay! I've come to give 'ee a dressin' down!

Dame (*to the audience*) Oo, girls! I knew my luck would change!

Captain This galley be a proper pig sty!

Dame Good! I want you to feel at home! Talking of pigs—what do you give
a pig with chilblains?—*Oinkment!* (*She roars with laughter*)

Captain (*roaring*) *Belay!* Our last cook kept the place spotless. You could
eat off the floor!

Dame Well, you can now! That's where most of the food ends up!

Captain *Food!* You call that binge you serve up, food!? All you've given us
so far is baked beans and rhubarb tart!

Dame Well, I like to give you a good run for your money.

Captain And another thing! You never wash yer utensils!

Dame Oh! That's a fib! I washed three pairs this morning! (*Very coy*) My
Sunday ones! I've just hung 'em from the crow's nest to dry!

Captain (*roaring*) *What!* Get 'em *down!*

Dame (*acting shocked*) Oooo! Captain! What a thing to say! (*Indicating the
Mate*) In front of the child too!

*Bellowing with rage, the Captain advances on her. The Dame ups with her
skirts and runs out* L, *pursued by enraged Captain*

Mate (*after a short pause, the penny has dropped*) Oinkment!

The Mate gives his crazy laugh and exits, removing the table

The Lights fade to Black-out

SCENE 4

The deck of the Golden Hawk

*Across the back are the bulwarks. The ship is Eastern in design and colourfully
painted. The wings represent masts, rigging and sails. There are barrels and
sea chests dotted about the deck and near the bulwarks. The backcloth shows
blue sky*

The Lights come up on Sinbad and the crew. They go straight into a jolly seafaring song and dance

8. Song (Sinbad and Chorus)

After the song, the Captain and Mate enter. The Captain has a large telescope under his arm. The Mate carries some rolled up sea charts

Captain Ship's Company!

All jump to attention

Be about yer dooties! Jump to it!
All Ay, Ay, Cap'n!

Sinbad and the crew run off

Captain Mister Mate!
Mate Yeth, Cap'n?
Captain 'Ave 'ee got the charts?
Mate Not thinth I've been takin' the medithine, Cap'n.
Captain *The charts,* you cloth-eared cuttle fish! The *sea* charts!
Mate Oh, thilly me!

He gives the charts to Captain who hands him the telescope

Captain 'Ere! Be doin' somethin' wi' that! (*He unrolls the chart and studies it*)

The Mate looks at the telescope then at the audience

Mate Er . . . Cap'n?
Captain Ar?
Mate What thall I do with it?
Captain (*to the audience*) Shall I tell 'im, shipmates? (*To the Mate*) You stick it up——
Mate (*jumping back*) Oh!!
Captain —to yer eye an' look fer land! (*He goes back to the chart*)
Mate Oh, yeth! I am a thilly thauthage! (*He scans the audience with the telescope*) Oo! Mm! Oo! (*He turns the telescope on the Captain and yells with fright*) Ahhh!
Captain (*still deep in his chart*) Can 'ee spy anything?
Mate Yeth! A big ugly thea monthter!
Captain (*looking up*) What?! (*He sees the Mate looking at him*) That be *me*, you barnacled buffoon!

He jabs the end of the telescope, hitting the Mate in the eye and making him fall over

Sinbad enters

Sinbad Any sign of land yet, Cap'n?
Captain Not a speck, lad.
Sinbad I hope we find Zalabar soon. The thought of my lovely Yasmin in the hands of that vile magician is driving me crazy!

Captain Don't 'ee worry, Sinbad. Accordin' to this chart, we should sight the island afore nightfall.

Sinbad (*desperately*) And what will happen then? How can *I* save her? What can *I* do against Vazar and his evil powers? Oh, I was stupid to even *think* I could rescue her! (*A deep sigh*)

Captain (*putting a friendly hand on Sinbad's shoulder*) Stow that talk! That bain't like our old Sinbad. Cheer up, me hearty.

Mate Yeth. You know what they alwayth thay——

The Mate and Captain burst into song

9. Song (Mate, Captain and Sinbad)

Very soon Sinbad shrugs off his gloom and joins them in the song

Sinbad Thanks, shipmates! You've cheered me up no end! Oh, I can't wait to get to grips with that mouldy old magician!

To suitable music, Dame Sinbad and Monty dance on hand in paw. The Dame wears an outrageous bathing costume and Monty wears baggy swimming shorts and water wings. The Crew enter and enjoy the comic capers. Dame and Monty go to the front edge of stage and do comic business of preparing to take a dive

Dame Sharon Davies, eat yer 'eart out! (*She holds her nose and is about to jump off the edge of the stage*)

Captain (*roaring at her*) Avast there!

Dame (*jumping back*) Oh! Captain! I wish you wouldn't *do* that! Cor! You've given me palpitations in me combinations! (*To the audience*) Do you like the outfit, folks? (*She does a twirl*) I got it from (*local shop*). It was on special offer. Yes. They paid *me* to take it away.

Captain What be you doin'?

Dame Monty an' me thought we'd go for a swim. (*Sidling up to him*) Why don't you get yer snorkel out and join me in a dip. (*Nudging him*) Who knows, it might turn out to be a *lucky dip*! (*She winks at him*)

Captain You can't swim 'ere. These are shark-infested waters.

Dame Oh, Captain! You're pullin' my leg!

Captain *Pull* it! I couldn't even *lift* it!

The Mate does his crazy laugh

All (*to him*) Shut up!

The laugh is cut dead

Dame (*to the Captain*) It's time I had a good look around this floatin' bath-tub of yours. I'll start at the blunt end.

Captain Stern! *Stern!*

Dame OK. (*In a very stern voice*) I'll start at the blunt end! (*Sweetly*) Was that stern enough for you?

Sinbad No, Mum. Aboard ship we call the blunt end the stern.

Dame Oh, I see. Then I'll go to the sharp end.

Captain Bow! *Bow!*

Dame Oh, you slave driver, you! (*She bows twice*) Bow! Bow! That better? (*To the audience*) Who does *he* think he is— (*topical gag*)?
Captain What be you doin' on deck anyway? Why ain't you below cookin' our lunch? You promised us fish and chips, didn't she, lads?
Crew Ay!
Dame I can't! No fish!
All No fish?
Dame There's no fish, no plaice! I cod you not!
Captain Then you'll 'ave to catch some!
Dame (*agog*) Me?
All *You!*
Dame But, I don't know 'ow!
Sinbad Don't worry, Mum. I'll catch some for you.
Dame Oh, there's a good boy! (*She takes Monty's paw*) Come on, Mr Shorthouse, let's go and titivate some taters!

The Dame and Monty exit. The Captain, Mate and Crew exit

Sinbad goes up to the bulwarks, takes a fishing line from a barrel, and throws it over the side. Holding the line, he sits on a barrel

Sinbad (*facing front*) Oh, Yasmin! I wish you could hear me. Just in case you can, I want you to know that I'm coming to save you. I love you so much. You're in my thoughts every minute of the day, and when I sleep, you fill my dreams. (*He sings*)

10. Song (Sinbad, Yasmin and Handmaidens)

When he starts to sing, the Lights fade leaving him in a spotlight. He finishes singing and falls asleep. The music continues and special "dream" lighting fills the stage. A little ground mist will add to the effect

Princess Yasmin and the Handmaidens float into the scene. Yasmin takes up the song as the girls dance round her. She finishes singing and vanishes into the mist with the Handmaidens

The music ends and the Lights return to normal. There is a sharp tug at the fishing line and Sinbad wakes with a start. He yawns. Another tug at the line

(*Jumping up*) A bite! I've got a bite! (*He pulls the line*) It's—it's a big 'un too! I can't manage it! (*Calling*) Ahoy! All hands on deck! Ahoy there!

The Captain, Mate and Crew rush on

I've hooked a big one, messmates! Lend a hand!

The Captain, Mate and some of the Crew form a chain behind Sinbad

Captain Haul away! *Heave! Heave!*

They heave at the line. Suddenly, there is a blinding flash and a great clap of thunder. The line snaps and Sinbad and the others are thrown backwards. The stage grows dark and eerie. Weird lights flicker from the sea and strange noises fill the air. Slowly, the huge, hideous head and neck of a Sea Serpent rises above the bulwarks

Barracuda's voice is heard on the offstage microphone. It should appear to be coming from the Serpent

Barracuda's Voice

Beware Sinbad, and listen to me!
I am Barracuda, the Witch of the Sea!
In the shape of a serpent I've come to call,
To show off my powers to one and all!
I know your mission, you meddlesome goon!
You hope to rescue the princess soon!
But I am here to stop your plan!
You'll never save her, try all you can!
I've come to put a curse on you,
And it's no use hiding in the loo!
Return at once to Old Baghdad,
Or suffer this curse, you foolish lad!

(*The Curse*)

May toothache keep you awake at night,
And all your underpants be tight!
May corns appear on your big toe!
And you sprout a nose like Barry Manilow!
May you lose at Bingo every time,
And be made to watch this pantomime!
May you shrink away and lose your stature,
And be forced to kiss old Maggie Thatcher!
These things will happen, believe you me,
If you remain upon the sea!

Sinbad (*leaping on to a chest near the bulwarks; defiantly to the Serpent*)

If Vazar has sent you to frighten me off,
Return and tell him I won't be put off!

(*He quickly takes something from his pouch*)

Here is something to make you depart!
A slice of my mum's rhubarb tart!

He forces the tart into the Serpent's mouth. With a roar, the Creature thrashes its head from side to side as if in pain. It gives a tremendous belch and sinks out of sight. The Lights return to normal

Crew Hurray! Good old Sinbad (*etc*)!

Sinbad I certainly dealt with that over-sized sprat! It'll have bellyache for weeks!

Captain 'Ave a care, Sinbad. If you'm still at sea tomorrow she'll feed 'ee to the sharks!

Sinbad But I won't be, will I? You said we'll be at Zalabar before nightfall.

Captain Ar! Let's 'ope I'm right! Mister Mate! Take a look through the spyglass. We *must* sight land soon.

Mate Yeth, Cap'n! (*He stands on a sea-chest and peers off* L, *through the telescope. Seeing something*) Oooh!

Captain See anythin'?

Mate Yeth!
Sinbad Is it land?
Mate No! Ith a thip!
Captain A thip?
Mate A thailing thip!
Captain A ship! Belay! (*He pulls the Mate down, grabs the telescope and mounting the chest, peers off* L) Tis a ship all right, an' ... bust me bobstays an' scuttle me scuppers! *She be flyin' the Jolly Roger!*
All Pirates!
Captain (*jumping down*) Men of the *Golden Hawk*! Arm yourselves! Cutlasses at the ready! Jump to it!

The Crew run out

The Mate, in a panic, hides inside or behind a large barrel

(*Looking through the telescope*) By thunder! 'Tis the Black Hook! The scurge of the Seven Sea! The worst pirate on the Spanish Main!
Mate (*popping up from barrel*) He'th ever tho nathty! (*He vanishes again*)
Sinbad They're coming alongside!

To suitable music, the pirate ship appears behind the bulwarks from UL. On deck, roaring and waving cutlasses, are an ugly band of Pirates. One waves the Skull and Crossbones flag. In their midst stands Black Hook himself. The Crew run on, armed with cutlasses

Black Hook (*bellowing*) Avast, there, ye lily livered swabs! Will 'ee yield to the Black Hook, or do we take 'ee by force! Surrender or *die*!

The Pirates roar and wave their swords

Captain (*to the Crew*) Do we surrender, lads?
Crew (*waving cutlasses*) No! We fight!
Captain (*calling back to Black Hook*) Listen to me, Black Hook! The first o' your bilge rats to set foot on my ship gets me cutlass through 'is gizzard!
Black Hook Prepare to die then! Board 'er, me buckos!
Captain Stand by to repel boarders!

To loud music and sea-battle noises, Black Hook and his men swarm on to the ship and fight with the Captain, Sinbad and Crew. If, practical, some Pirates can swing in from the wings on ropes. A Pirate pulls the Mate from his hiding place and chases him around. At last, Black Hook disarms the Captain and forces him to his knees

Black Hook (*bellowing above the din*) Belay! Ye swabs! Belay!

The others pause in their fight

Surrender, you scurvy scum, or I'll cover the deck with this swab's entrails! (*He jabs the Captain with his hook*)
Captain Fight on lads, fight on!

But Sinbad and the Crew drop their swords

Black Hook (*planting his foot on the Captain and waving his hook*) Har har! Victory! The *Golden Hawk* be ours! Ha har! (*He kicks the Captain over*)

The Pirates cheer. They herd Sinbad and Crew R. *Two Pirates, Yellow Jack and Blue Peter, drag the Captain and Mate* L

1st Pirate (*pointing to Sinbad and the Crew*) Wot shall us do wi 'em, Cap'n?
2nd Pirate Make 'em walk the plank!
Pirates Ay!
3rd Pirate 'Ang 'em from the yard-arm!
Pirates Ay!
4th Pirate Send 'em to (*local place*)!
Pirates Too cruel! Too cruel!
Black Hook Belay! *I* be Cap'n 'ere! I'll decide what's to be done wi 'em! (*He inspects Sinbad and the Crew*) This lot'll fetch a fine price at the Zalabar slave market. We'll take 'em there and sell 'em!
Yellow Jack (*pushing the Captain and Mate forward*) Reckon we could sell these two, Cap'n?

Black Hook inspects the Captain and Mate. The latter is shaking with fright

Black Hook Sell 'em!? By Blackbeard's ghost, I couldn't *give* 'em away! Throw 'em over the side an' let the sharks 'ave 'em! Ha har!

The Pirates cheer as the Captain and Mate are dragged to the back and pushed over the side. Loud splashes are heard and the Pirates cheer again. Sinbad pulls free and lunges at Black Hook

Sinbad You murderous dog, I'll——

Black Hook pushes Sinbad back to the Pirates, who grab him

Black Hook Get back or I'll rip yer liver an' lights out! (*He brandishes his hook*)
Blue Peter Three cheers for the Black Hook! Hip hip!
Pirates Hurray!
Peter Hip hip!
Pirates Hurray!

Dame Sinbad and Monty bounce on L, *blissfully unaware of what has happened*

Peter Hip hip!
Dame }
Pirates } (*together*) Hurray!
Dame (*dancing with Monty and singing*) "For he's a jolly good fellow! For he's a jolly good fellow! For he's a jolly good fellow—and so say all of us." (*To the audience*) Everyone seems happy! Is it someone's birthday? I thought I 'eard a bit of a party goin' on. (*She sees Sinbad and goes to him*) Hello Sinny! Hey! What's up with you? You've got a face like (*local place*) on a wet weekend! What's up with ya?

Black Hook has moved behind Dame and Monty. The monkey sees him and tries to attract Dame's attention by pulling at her skirts

(*Pushing Monty away*) Stop doin' that you cheeky chimp! (*To Sinbad*) Why aren't you enjoyin' the party? Did someone swipe yer ice cream?

Monty pulls at her skirt

Oh, give over, you bad baboon!

Monty points at Black Hook. The Dame looks and does a huge double-take

(*To the audience*) Don't look now, but (*TV villain or pop star*) is here!

Black Hook (*bellowing at her*) I am the Black Hook!

Dame Yes! You look as if you could do with a wash!

Black Hook (*snarling and brandishing his hook*) Ahhggr!

Monty jumps into the Dame's arms

I'm the *blackest—blood thirstiest—brutalest—*Buccaneer on the Briny! Ha har! Ha har! Ha har!

Dame (*to Sinbad*) Who's yer funny friend?

Sinbad He's no friend of mine! He's taken the ship, thrown the captain overboard, and he's going to sell us in the slave market!

Dame (*wailing and falling to her knees*) Oh, no! Please don't sell *me*, Mr Black Puddin'! I'm not worth anything! I've gone over my sell-by date! (*She clings to his leg*) Oh, don't sell me! I'm only a poor, defenceless girl!

Black Hook Ye'll be sold along wi' the rest! Just think, by this time tomorrow, you could be in the hareem of some foreign prince! Used as his plaything!

She stops wailing and gives a big grin

Dame Could I? (*She jumps up and preens herself. To the audience*) It doesn't sound so bad after all, does it, girls?

Black Hook (*to the Pirates*) Take the prisoners below an' clap 'em in irons!

Some of the Pirates drag Sinbad, Monty and the Crew out

The Dame is the last to go

Dame (*to a small Pirate who is pushing her*) 'Ere! Don't you manhandle me, you pint-sized pip-squeak!

The Pirate jabs her in the rear with his cutlass

Ooo! All right, I get your *point*! (*To the audience*) I shall complain about this to (*local town councillor or well-known public figure*).

The Pirate pushes the Dame out

Black Hook (*to the Pirates*) Avast there, me brave buckos! Make merry! Bring grog! Our next stop be the slave market at Zalabar! Ha har!

Pirates Hurray!

11. Song (Pirates)

This should be a rollicking Pirate song and dance. It ends with Black Hook standing on a sea-chest waving the Skull and Crossbones. The Pirates form a tableau around him, and on the last note of music——

—the CURTAIN *falls*

blue curtain closed.

ACT II

SCENE 1

Above the Valley of Skulls

Tabs or frontcloth as used in Act I, Scene 2. Eerie lighting and sinister music

Vazar enters

Vazar (*to the audience, with mocking bows*) Salaams and greetings, my little camel droppings! Did you all enjoy the break? Did you have a nice time stuffing yourselves with sweets and crisps? Good! (*With evil relish*) Well, I hope you all get the bellyache! Ha! Ha! Ha! (*Looking off*) Ah! Here comes Barracuda! I can't wait to hear how she scared the pants off Sinbad the Sailor!

Barracuda enters looking glum and holding her belly

          O Mighty Witch of All the Sea!
          Have you got some good news for me?

Barracuda   Alas, the news I bring is bad!
          I had no luck with young Sinbad!
          He forced me to eat some rhubarb tart!
          Which made me sick and made me—feel very poorly!

(*She groans and rubs her belly*)
          If he were still upon the sea,
          I'd do him in most hideously!

Vazar   Not at sea? What mean you by that?
          Tell me! Where is the confounded brat!?

Barracuda   His ship was seized by a pirate band,
          And he's now their prisoner on dry land!
          And as you know my magic thins,
          Where water ends and land begins!

Vazar   I hope the pirates slaughter him!
          I hope they tear him limb from limb!

Barracuda   'Tis not their plan to kill the knave!
          They're going to sell him as a slave!

Vazar   Then I must away and kill the toad!
              Before to some goody-goody he is sold!
              Tell me, Witch, where is the sale?
              I'll go at once, and shall not fail!

(*He takes out his evil-looking dagger*)

Barracuda You need not look so very far,
               The sale is here in Zalabar!
               And as the auction starts at ten,
               You'd better get your skates on then!

Vazar (*to the audience, brandishing the dagger*)
               Of Sinbad the Sailor you'll see no more,
               When this dagger strikes true and sure!
               I'll slice him up, and cut him in two,
               And when I've done that—I'll come down there for you!
               Ha Ha! To the slave market!

They laugh demoniacally, and exit

The Lights fade to a Black-out

b   c   o

SCENE 2

The Slave Market

Across the back runs an Eastern-style wall with a practical archway in the centre. The backcloth shows sand and palm trees. Prominent R *is an inn with a signboard reading,* "Ye Olde Camel's Hump". *The wings represent houses and alleyways. There is a rostrum set* LC, *with a sign over it that reads:* "Super Slave Sale Today"

Eastern-type music to set the scene. The Lights come up on a crowd of Townsfolk. The music changes quickly to the Pirates' song

Black Hook and his men emerge from the inn, singing lustily

12. Song (Pirates)

This can be a reprise of Song 11 or a new song. After the song, Black Hook mounts the rostrum

Black Hook People of Zalabar! Pay heed to the Black Hook! 'Ave yer pieces o' eight ready, 'cos the slave auction is about to begin! But first, to wet the gentlemen's appetites—bring on the dancin' girls!

Some shapely and scantly-clad Belly Dancers run from the inn and perform their exotic dance

The Pirates whoop and cheer

13. Dance (Belly Dancers)

After the dance, the girls run out L

The Pirates clap and cheer

And now 'tis time for the slave sale to begin! Bring in the merchandise!

Peter and Jack exit L

Roll up! Roll up! Roll up for the slave sale of the century! Come an' get yer slaves 'ere! Roll up! Roll up!

Peter and Jack return dragging Sinbad, Monty, and Dame Sinbad. She wears a voluminous gown which covers her comic striptease outfit

Sinbad and Monty get on to the rostrum, but the Dame holds back. The two Pirates start pushing her

Dame Stop pushin'! You'll disarrange me duvet! (*Business with the gown*)
Jack (*pushing her on to the rostrum*) Get up there!
Black Hook 'Ere they be! The finest slaves this side o' (*local place*)!
Dame Cor! 'Ark at him, name dropping!
Black Hook (*growling at her*) Arrrrgh!
Dame (*growling back*) Arrrrgh, yerself, you old video nasty, you! (*Waving to the audience*) Hello, folks! (*She gets down from the rostrum and comes forward to have a chat with the audience*)

Black Hook, outraged, follows her down

Nice to see you all again! We've been havin' a terrible time! You just can't imagine! These perishin' pirates 'ave treated us somethin' chronic! I'm black and blue all over! I've got a bruise 'ere——
Black Hook (*roaring at her*) Stow that bilge!
Dame Listen, Mr Black and Decker! It's very rude to interrupt. Go and splice yer mainbrace if you want somethin' to do! (*Back to the audience*) Now, as I was sayin'——
Black Hook (*grabbing hold of her*) Shut yer trap or I'll rip yer liver and lights out! (*Thrusting his hook under her nose*) Wi' this!
Dame You know what you can do with *that*, don't ya?
Black Hook What?
Dame Go and—pick yer nose with it! (*To the audience*) Ha! Ha! That's tellin' 'im!

With a bellow, Black Hook clamps his hook round her throat

(*Gurgling*) I—I didn't mean it! I think you're the *salt* of the earth.
Black Hook (*releasing her, flattered*) You *do*?
Dame Yes. What a pity you left the cellar!

She, Sinbad, Monty and the Townsfolk roar with laughter

Black Hook (*enraged*) Belay, ye swabs! I mean to sell you slaves today! I'll stoop to any lengths!
Dame What, in *them* knickers?!

Black Hook (*dragging her back to the rostrum*) On wi' the sale! (*To the Townsfolk*) Who'll start the bidding? (*Pulling Sinbad out of the line up*) What be I bid for this. 'Ere's a strong, capable lad! (*To Sinbad*) Show 'em yer muscles!

Dame Don't you show 'em anything, Sinny!

Black Hook (*holding up Sinbad's arm*) Muscles like iron! Who'll start the biddin' at two dinars? Two dinars, anyone?

1st Man Two dinars!

Black Hook Any advance on two dinars?

Dame Yes! Three dinars with ice-cream to follow!

Black Hook (*to the crowd*) Do I hear three dinars?

2nd Man Three dinars!

1st Woman Four dinars!

3rd Man Five dinars!

Black Hook Ho! Ho! This be more like it. Five dinars, I'm bid. Who'll say six?

No takers

Goin' fer five dinars then! Goin'—Goin'——

Sinbad Stop! You can't sell me! I'm a free man!

Dame Atta boy!

Monty (*beating his chest*) Oo! Oo!

Sinbad jumps down from the rostrum

Sinbad (*to all*) I was born free and that's the way I'm going to stay! (*He sings*)

14. Song (Sinbad, Chorus)

This can be a solo number or everyone can join in, even the Pirates!

Black Hook (*coming down to Sinbad*) Stow that mutinous talk, dog! (*To the Crowd*) Take no notice. 'E got ideas above 'is station. A good lash o' the whip will cure 'im! (*To 3rd Man*) You bid five dinars. 'E be yours, I reckon.

3rd Man Huh! I don't want him! He's too full of himself. He'd start giving *me* orders! You keep him!

With a growl, Black Hook pushes Sinbad back on to the rostrum and points out the Dame

Black Hook Next we 'ave *this* . . . this captivatin' creature! See 'ow elegant she walks! (*Growling at her*) Walk, you old cod fish!

He pushes her off the rostrum and she lands with a thump on her rump

Dame Ahh! Cor! I landed right on me rumpus! (*To the Crowd*) I'm shop soiled now. You can get me cheap!

Black Hook (*bellowing at her*) Walk!

She jumps up and parades up and down in comic mannequin fashion

(*Doing his best*) "She walks in beauty like the night ..."

Dame (*wiggling as she walks*) This flippin' corset's much too tight!

Black Hook Look at that hour-glass figure!

Dame (*walking bowlegged*) What a shame all the sand's gone to the bottom.

Black Hook jumps from the rostrum and grabs her

Black Hook Stop tryin' to make a fool out of me!

Dame I never interfere with nature, old son!

Black Hook Make the best of yourself!

Dame I can't! I've got furniture trouble!

Black Hook Furniture trouble?

Dame Yes! Me *chest* has fallen into me *drawers*!

Black Hook Show 'em yer assets!

Dame Oh! Don't be so rude!

Black Hook Show 'em yer teeth!

She gives the crowd a toothy grin

Teeth like stars!

Dame Yeah! They come out at night!

Black Hook What be I bid for this fine fragment of female flesh? Who'll say half a dinar?

Townsfolk (*in disgust*) No thanks! Keep her! Yuck! (*Etc.*)

Black Hook (*hauling the Dame to one side*) You'd better do summit to attract 'em, or I'm goin' to rip yer liver an' lights out! (*He makes slashing gestures with the hook across her belly*)

Dame Ooh! All right, Mr Black Label! I'll do somethin'! (*The Prima Donna*) I shall perform my *neurotic* dance!

Black Hook Don't you mean *exotic*?

Dame You ain't seen it yet! Music! Lights! Action!

15. Comic Striptease (Dame)

The music starts and Dame Sinbad performs her comic striptease with special lighting. Under her gown are layers of corsets, bras, frilly knickers, etc. As she discards each item she throws it to Black Hook. To finish, she wears bloomers with two big hand prints on the seat and a T-shirt with a comic slogan across the chest. She strikes a pose on the last note of music. The lighting returns to normal

The Townsfolk rush out in disgust

Black Hook (*enraged*) You old trout! You've frightened all the customers away! (*He dumps the clothes into the Dame's arms*) Well, you 'ad yer chance an' lost it! (*To Jack and Peter*) Bring 'em 'ere, lads!

The two Pirates drag Sinbad and Monty down from the rostrum

Black Hook Nobody's goin' to buy you three swabs, so—I be goin' to rip yer liver an' lights out! (*He advances on them, brandishing his hook*)

The Dame hides behind Sinbad and Monty hides behind her

Dame Oh, do somethin', Sinny, or 'e'll put our insides on the outside!

Sinbad Listen, Black Hook. Try selling us again. If you kill us now you'll get nothing. Better sell us for just a few dinars than return to your ship emptyhanded.

Monty (*to Hook, nodding his head*) Oo! Oo!

Black Hook (*rubbing his chin with his hook*) Mm . . . ar! You'm right! I'll give 'ee a second chance.

The three give a sigh of relief

But, be warned! If you ain't sold by three o'clock, I'll——

Sinbad ⎫   ⎧ Rip yer liver and lights out!
Dame ⎬ (*together*) ⎨ Rip yer liver and lights out!
Monty ⎭   ⎩ Oo! Oo! Oo! Oo! Oo! Oo!

Black Hook You got it! (*To Jack and Peter*) Put 'em in that pen yonder! (*He points off* L) And make sure they be tied up good an' tight. When you've done that, join us at the inn fer a bucket o' grog!

Jack and Peter start dragging them out DL

Dame (*to Hook, as she goes*) Can I come? I could murder a pint!

Jack, Peter, Sinbad, Monty and Dame exit DL *and Black Hook and the Pirates exit into the inn*

A slight pause, then Vazar appears in the centre archway

Vazar (*coming down and looking about him*) Strange, very strange! The place is empty! (*To the audience*) Is the slave sale over? Is it early closing day? Well! Why don't you answer me, you rude riff-raff!

The audience are suitably rude

Bah! Any more of that, and I'll turn you all into human beings!

Jack and Peter enter DL

(*Bowing; very oily*) Salaams and greetings! Could you tell me if the slave sale is over for today?

Jack 'Tis open again after lunch.

Vazar How many slaves have already been sold?

Peter None! (*To Jack*) Let's get to the grog!

They move to the inn. Vazar stops them

Vazar Tell me, is one permitted to view the merchandise before the auction?

Jack Ar! They be in that pen over there. (*He points* L)

Peter Go take a look. You'll think twice about buyin' 'em when you do!

Laughing, Peter and Jack exit into the inn

Vazar (*to the audience*) Ha! Ha! Ha! I'm not going to *buy* them, I'm going to *kill* them! (*He takes out a dagger*) Soon Sinbad will be out of my way forever! (*He creeps* DL, *and looks off*) Ah, yes! I can see him! All tied up! Ready for the slaughter! (*He brandishes the dagger, about to exit*)

Black Hook enters from the inn, carrying a huge tankard

Black Hook (*booming at Vazar*) Avast there!!

Vazar (*quickly concealing the dagger*) Salaams and greetings!

Black Hook My men just told me you be wantin' to buy slaves. I be startin'
the auction again after lunch. (*He holds up the tankard*) Come an' 'ave a
drop o' lunch wi' me!

Vazar But, I have to . . . (*He moves to the exit* DL)

Black Hook (*planting his hook on Vazar's shoulder*) Never refuse the Black
Hook, if you know what's good fer 'ee! (*He glares at Vazar, then drinks*)

Vazar (*to the audience*) Curses! It now seems I have to *buy* Sinbad before I
can kill him!

Black Hook (*dragging Vazar to the inn*) Come on, me bucko! The first barrel
is on me!

Black Hook pushes Vazar into the inn and follows him off

Slight pause

*The Captain appears in the archway and creeps downstage. He wears an
Arab costume and a large false beard*

Captain (*to the audience*) Ahoy, shipmates! 'Tis me, the cap'n! Oh! (*He pulls
down the beard*) That be better. I bet you thought we was gonners, eh?
Well, we give the sharks the slip and swam ashore. We got 'old o' these
Arab nighties, an' we'm 'ere to rescue young Sinbad. Ain't we, Mister
Mate? (*He discovers he is alone*) Bust me bobstays! Where *is* the crazy
cuttle fish! (*He goes to the archway; calling off*) Mister Mate!

Mate (*off*) Thith way! *Thith way!*

*The Mate appears in the archway wearing a very long Arab costume and an
enormous false beard. He is gesturing madly to something off stage*

Thith way! Come here, you thilly thauthage!

Captain (*pushing him aside*) Leave this to me! (*Calling off*) This be your
captain hollerin'! Forward march! Left, right! Left, right! Left, right!

*To suitable music, a charming Camel trots in through the archway and does
a comic canter around the stage*

Halt!

*The Camel's front legs come to a sudden halt, but the back ones don't, and it
concertinas up in the middle*

At ease!

*The back end of the Camel sits down on the ground. After some comic
manœuvres, the Captain and Mate succeed in getting the back end to stand up.
They lead the Camel forward, where it stands with its legs crossed*

(*To the audience*) Ain't she nice, shipmates? I wonder what 'er name is?

The Camel whispers in his ear

Oh, that be a pretty name! Shall I tell the boys and girls?

The Camel shakes her head and whispers in the Mate's ear. Comic business being tickled

Mate (*to the audience*) Thea thayth thea wanth you to geth her name.
Captain Guess 'er name. Right! (*To the audience*) Now, me hearties, if you guess 'er name right, she'll nod 'er head like this——

The Camel nods her head

An' if you guess wrong she'll shake her head like that——

The Camel shakes her head

Cor! Ain't she intelligent? I bet she don't go to (*local school*)! Right, shipmates, let's 'ear 'ee shout out what you think 'er name be.

The audience shout out various names. The Camel stamps her foot and whispers to the Mate

Mate (*to the Captain*) Thea thayth thea can't 'ear clear.
Captain Can't 'ear clear? Must be all the sand in 'er lugholes!

The Camel whispers to him

Ar! (*To the audience*) She says she'd 'ear clear if you was 'ere near. In other words, she wants some of 'ee to come up an' stand beside 'er. Now, who be comin' up?

The House Lights come up. The children come up on to the stage. The Captain and Mate get them to say what they think the Camel's name is. The Camel shakes her head

(*Bringing the last child to the Camel*) Now, 'ere's the last little boy/girl. (*To the child*) What do you think 'er name is?

The child says a name. If it is already given, the Captain will have to ad lib and get the child to try another name. The Camel nods her head vigorously and dances for joy

Captain (*to the child*) You've guessed right, shipmate! 'Er name be Daisy (*or whatever*)! An' what's your name?

The child tells him

Well done, (*name*). (*To the audience*) Let's give (*name*) a great big clap!

The Captain, Mate and audience applaud. The Camel stamps her foot

(*Bringing all the children forward*) Let's give 'em all a great big clap!

They do so

The Mate gets sweets from off stage and hands them out to the children

When the children have returned to their seats, the House Lights go down

Mate (*to the Camel*) Can I have a kith? (*He puckers up his lips*)

The Camel jumps in the air and gallops off

Captain Back to the plot! What a bit o' luck Black Hook brought Sinbad to
Zalabar. For tis on this very island that Vazar 'olds the princess captive!
What a stroke o' luck, eh, Mister Mate?

Mate (*to the audience*) Yeth, and it cut'th down on the thenery ath well! (*He
gives them a wink*)

Captain But where *is* Sinbad? (*To the audience*) Mates, do *you* know where
he is?

Audience: "He's out there", etc.

Out 'ere? (*He goes* DL *and looks off*) By thunder! They be right! There's
young Sinbad an' the others, all trussed up like Matthews Turkeys! To the
rescue!

They are about to exit as:

Black Hook enters from the inn, followed by Jack and Peter

Black Hook (*roaring at them*) Avast there!

Captain (*in a quick aside to the Mate*) Yer beard!

They pull up their false beards and do their best to appear like Arabs

Black Hook What be you doin' 'ere, you scum of the desert?

Captain (*with a bad Arabian accent*) Salaam, O Prince of Pirates! I am . . . er
. . . Mustapha Fag and this is . . . er . . . Sheik Alego! I wish to buy slaves
from you, Effendi.

Black Hook Ho! Ho! Things be lookin' up! (*To the Pirates*) *Two* eager
customers, lads!

Captain *Two*, Effendi?

Black Hook Ay! There be another one who wants to buy me slaves. 'Ere he
comes now.

Vazar enters from the inn

The Captain and Mate go into a huddle. Black Hook talks with Vazar

Captain 'Tis Vazar, the magician! 'E be up to no good, for sure. He mustn't
get 'is claws on Sinbad. We'll have to outbid him in the sale!

Mate But, Cap'n, we ain't got no money to bid with.

Black Hook (*booming*) Roll up! Roll up! Roll up for the second part of the
slave auction! Roll up! Roll up!

The Townsfolk enter

(*To Jack and Peter*) Bring 'em in.

Jack and Peter exit L

(*To Vazar and the Captain*) Well, 'tis between you two who gets me slaves.
May the best man win, an' let 'im be a good payer-up—(*he brandishes his
hook*)—or else!

Vazar moves DR. *The Captain and Mate are* DL

Jack and Peter enter dragging Sinbad, the Dame and Monty. The Dame is now wearing a comic tattered costume. They are dragged C

'Ere they be! The best slaves that money can buy!

Vazar turns to look

Dame (*seeing him*) Ah! Look! It's Dirty Bertie (*or TV villain*) again!
Sinbad *You!* What have you done with Princess Yasmin? I'll . . . (*He rushes at Vazar*)
Black Hook (*pushing him back*) Get back, ye swab, or I'll rip yer liver and lights out! (*He talks with Vazar*)
Captain (*whispering loudly*) Sinbad!

Sinbad looks at the Captain who quickly pulls down his beard

Shh!
Black Hook On wi' the sale. I be goin' to sell these slaves as a lot. Who'll start the bidding at ten dinars?
Vazar Ten!
Captain Eleven!
Vazar Twelve!
Captain Thirteen!
Vazar Fourteen!

Pause, while the Mate urges the Captain not to go any higher

Black Hook Any advance on fourteen dinars? Goin' fer fourteen dinars! Goin'—Goin'——
Captain Fourteen and a quarter!
Vazar Bah! Enough of this! (*He takes a bulging money bag from his sash*) I have in this bag, *one hundred dinar!* I will pay it *all* for the slaves! (*Waving the bag at Hook*) Is it a bargain?
Black Hook (*going to him; eagerly*) Ay! Tis a bar——
Captain Wait! I . . . I have one hundred and *one* dinar!
Vazar He lies! Demand to see it! (*He puts the bag back into his sash*)
Black Hook Ar! That be fair! (*Going to the Captain*) Let's see the colour of yer money!
Captain (*a strangled croak*) Now?
Black Hook (*bellowing*) Now!

The Captain pretends to search his robes for the non-existent money. Black Hook looms over him. Vazar, sneering, turns away. Monty, on whispered instructions from Sinbad, creeps over to Vazar and gingerly takes the money bag from his sash. He creeps around behind Black Hook, and puts the bag into the Mate's hand then scuttles back to Sinbad. The dumbfounded Mate nudges the Captain and shows him the bag

Captain (*seizing it and forgetting his Arab accent*) Why, shiver me timbers! . . . er . . . I mean—(*Arab accent*) Allah be praised! (*To Black Hook*) Here it is, Effendi! My one hundred and one dinar! (*He gives the bag to Black Hook*)

Vazar spins round, sees the bag and looks for his own

Vazar That's *my* bag! I've been robbed!

All react

Black Hook But, 'e just ... (*To the Captain*) By Blackbeard's ghost! I'll rip yer liver an' lights out! (*He advances on the Captain*)
Captain (*yelling*) Abandon ship!

The Captain and Mate run out DL

Black Hook After the swabs!
Vazar *Hold!* Why waste your time with those fools. Keep the hundred dinar. I still want the slaves. Is it a bargain?
Black Hook Ay! 'Tis a bargain! Give 'im the slaves!

Jack and Peter push Sinbad and the others over to Vazar

Vazar (*aside to Sinbad*) At last! Once away from here, I'm going to finish you off for good, sailor boy! (*Aloud*) Come, my slaves!
Black Hook Belay! You can't take 'em yet!
Vazar Why not? I've paid for them!
Black Hook Ar! But there be a tradition wi' us pirates. Anyone who buys slaves from us must enjoy our 'ospitality. You must come an' take grog wi' me!
Vazar Some other time!

Dragging Sinbad, Vazar goes to exit R, *but finds Jack and Peter barring his way with drawn cutlasses*

Black Hook Never break a pirate tradition! Lads! Take 'em to me tent!

Jack and Peter drag Sinbad and the others out DR

Dame (*to the audience as she goes*) 'Ere we go again!

The Dame exits

Vazar (*to the audience*) Curses! Foiled again!

Black Hook clamps his hook on Vazar and hauls him out, DR

Music starts and the Pirates burst from the inn with the Belly Dancers

16. Dance or Song (Belly Dancers, Pirates or Camel)

This can be a reprise of the Pirate song or a dance for Pirates and Dancers— or, perhaps the Camel could trot on and give a solo performance. After the number, the Lights fade to Black-out

SCENE 3

On the way to Black Hook's tent

Tabs, or frontcloth showing the desert with palm trees and tents in the distance

To suitable music, Jack enters DR, *leading Sinbad, Monty and Dame. The three are linked together by a rope like a chain gang. Peter brings up the rear with drawn cutlass. The Dame stops, shattered and out of puff*

Peter (*snarling at her*) Get movin', droopy drawers!
Dame Oh, shut up! Niggle knickers!

Black Hook and Vazar enter DR

Ah Mr Black Stuff! How much further *is* it to your tatty ole tent?
Black Hook Round the bend!
Dame I know you are, but how far is it to your wigwam? I'm proper pooped!
Black Hook Move! or I'll rip yer liver an' lights out!
Dame (*to the audience*) I wish someone would put 'is *blinkin' lights out!*
Black Hook Move!

Jack pulls on the rope, and drags the three out DL. *Peter prods the Dame with cutlass as they go. Black Hook follows them out*

Vazar (*pausing at the exit, to the audience*) Ha! Ha! It won't be long now! (*He shows his dagger*) Once I get him away from this nit wit of a pirate, Sinbad will trouble me no more!

Vazar exits DL

The Captain and Mate creep on DR. *They still wear their Arab costumes, without beards*

Captain 'Ear that, Mister Mate! 'E be goin' to kill young Sinbad!
Mate What we goin' to do, Cap'n?
Captain Somehow, we've got to get into Black Hook's tent. But *how*? By thunder! If only we 'ad some disguises!

Two of the shapely Belly Dancers slink on DR. *They stop and eye the men flirtingly. The Mate sees them first and ogles them*

Hey, look at them two!
Mate (*drooling*) I'm lookin'!
Captain They give me an idea.
Mate (*pawing at the ground with his foot*) Me too! Cor! (*He is about to rush at the girls*)
Captain (*pushing him back*) Belay! *I* be Cap'n! I'll 'andle this!
Mate (*to the audience*) Thpoil thport!
Captain (*to the girls*) Top o' the mornin', ladies.

The girls giggle and slink around him

1st Girl (*sidling up*) 'Allo, big and 'andsome boy!
2nd Girl You stranger to theez parts, no? (*She moves in very close*)
Captain (*gulping*) I . . . er . . . ar!

The girls giggle and drift over to the Mate. They fawn over him, running their fingers through his hair, blowing in his ear and tickling him under the chin. He is in paradise and just stands there with a big soppy grin on his face

1st Girl Mm! Me like you! You sweetykins!

2nd Girl Leetle sweetykins! You nice leetle boy.

Captain (*to the audience*) How do 'ee like that! An' *I* be the captain! (*Bellowing at the Mate*) Mister Mate! Put down them Turkish Delights an' come 'ere! Mister Mate!

Mate (*rushing to the Captain*) Yeth, Cap'n?

Captain (*taking him aside*) Listen. I reckon they can be of use to us.

Mate (*ogling the girls*) Cor! You can thay that again!

Captain Stow that! We've got to get some new disguises. Ask 'em if they can lay their 'ands on anythin'. (*Pushing him over*) Ask 'em!

Mate (*to the girls*) Can—can you lay your handth on anythin'?

Girls (*giggling*) Ooo! Sweetykins! (*They move to him*)

Captain (*pulling the Mate away*) Not *you*! We want 'em to get us some clothes! (*Pushing him over*) Ask 'em!

Mate (*to the girls*) Can—can we get thome clotheth off you?

Girls Ooo! Naughty sweetykins!

Captain (*pushing the Mate aside*) Belay! (*To the girls*) Now, ladies, me an' Mister Mate 'ere be goin' to a fancy dress party, an' we'm wantin' some clothes to dress up in. Could 'ee get us some?

1st Girl Oh, we got no time now!

2nd Girl We got to do de dancin' for Black 'Ook de pirate!

1st Girl In eez tent. 'E beat us if we late!

2nd Girl We go now! We got zee runs now!

They wave to the Mate, giggle, and slink to the exit DL

Captain (*stopping them*) Ladies! Did you say you was dancin' fer Black Hook?

Girls Yees!

Captain Now? This minute?

Girls Yees!

Captain Ar! Well . . . er . . . we'll walk along with 'ee. You never know what villains be about. Some would steal the very clothes off your back! (*Aside to the Mate*) Come on, sweetykins! We'm goin' dancin'!

The Captain links arms with the girls and leads them off DL

Left alone, the Mate looks very upset

Giggling, the girls run back on and grab him

To suitable music, they dance him round and he does his crazy laugh

They dance off DL *as:*

The Lights fade to a Black-out

SCENE 4

Black Hook's tent

The main entrance is UC. *Drapes or a cut cloth can be used. The wings are draped to represent a tent interior.* UR, *across the corner, is a dais with a seat or divan*

*Sinbad, Monty and the Dame are being pushed into the tent by Jack and Peter.
The Dame trips and falls on her rear. The two Pirates roar with laughter and
exit* C

Dame (*yelling after them*) You clumsy clots! Oh! I'm fed up with bein'
pushed around! (*Groaning*) Oo! I think I've buckled me big end and
dented me dipstick!

They help her up

Sinny, do you really think that murky magician means to do us a nasty?
Sinbad Oh, he means it all right!
Dame Oh, we should never 'ave left 'ome! Never again will I see my little
house with the roses round the front—an' the bailiffs round the back! (*In
tears*) Oh! How could you do this to your poor old mother!
Sinbad You wanted to come on the voyage, Mum. I didn't force you.
Dame (*in a huff*) Oh, I see! Like that, is it! You don't want me here! Typical!
After all I've done for you! I've worked me fingers to the bone, and what
'ave I got to show for it—bony fingers! (*To the audience*) Flippin' kids!
Who'd 'ave 'em! (*To Sinbad*) You're a selfish young so and so, Sinbad!
Sinbad I'm not, Mum. I don't care what happens to me. I just want to save
my darling Yasmin. She's all I care about.
Dame (*sniffing*) And—and what about your Mummy? Don't you care
about 'er?
Sinbad (*putting his arm around her*) Of course I care about you. You're the
best mum in the world! I wouldn't be without you for anything. We
belong together, like—peaches and cream!
Dame Rhubarb and custard!
Sinbad Marks and Spencer!
Dame Dot and Charlie (*or popular TV/musical duo*)!

17. Song (Sinbad, Dame and Monty)

*A song and dance routine involving comic antics from Monty. After the song,
Sinbad hugs and kisses the Dame. Monty follows suit with comic business*

Oh, give over, you big soft nellies! Oh, but, what are we goin' to do, Sinny!
I'm too young to die! (*Very dramatic*) My days are numbered! My end is
nigh!

Monty peers at her bottom

Not *that* end, you furry fool!
Sinbad I might be able to save us yet. I'm going to bargain with Black
Hook. Don't give up, Mum. Where's your get up and go?
Dame It got up an' went!

Black Hook and Vazar enter C, *followed by Jack and Peter*

Don't look now, but Maggie and Dennis are 'ere!
Sinbad (*to Hook, pointing at Vazar*) *He* has kidnapped Princess Yasmin of
Baghdad. If you were to help us rescue her, the sultan would reward you
handsomely. Thousands of dinars! What do you say?
Black Hook (*stroking his chin with the hook*) Mm . . . 'tis a temptin' offer.

Vazar Don't listen to him, my friend. You have been robbing the sultan's ships for years! You are a wanted man. There is a bounty on your head.

Dame Yeah, an' a Mars bar in his ear'ole!

Vazar The sultan would have you beheaded the moment you set foot in Baghdad. That young dog is trying to trick you.

Black Hook You're right! (*Advancing on Sinbad*) I'll rip yer liver and lights out!

Vazar Wait! He is *my* slave now, remember. Let *me* remove him from your sight!

Black Hook Not yet. Remember the pirate tradition! You must enjoy me 'ospitality afore you takes 'em!

Vazar Oh, very well. But make it fast!

Black Hook Yellow Jack!

Jack Ay, Cap'n?

Black Hook Go an' tell the little darlin's we be ready fer 'em.

Jack runs out C

Blue Peter!

Peter Ay, Cap'n?

Black Hook Take the slaves to the other end of the tent an' tie 'em up!

Peter pushes Sinbad, the Dame and Monty out L

Dame (*as she goes*) Oh, no not again!

The Dame exits

Black Hook (*taking Vazar up to a seat on the dais*) Come an' sit down, me bucko.

They sit

I 'ave a very special treat in store for 'ee!

Jack enters C

Jack The dancin' girls, Cap'n. (*He stands to one side*)

The Captain enters C. *He is wearing a comic duplicate of the Belly Dancer's costume with female wig and yashmak. He strikes an awkward pose, then realizing he is on his own, he goes out again and pulls on the Mate. He is also wearing Belly Dancer's costume with wig and yashmak. They slink down and strike poses*

Black Hook (*jumping to his feet, roaring*) Great buckets o' blood! (*He storms over to the Captain*) What be this? You ain't the girls I hired!

Captain (*in a shaky falsetto*) A thousand pardons, O mighty one! Other girls sick. We substitutes.

Black Hook You look more like *substandards* to me!

Captain (*wiggling his belly*) I am Fatima!

Black Hook You can say that again! (*He pokes the Captain in belly with his hook. He moves to the Mate and likes what he sees*) Ar! Now this be more like it! And what might your name be, my little persian rose?

Mate (*very coy*) I am Thweetykinth!
Black Hook Ha har! You'm right there!

He leers at the Mate, who flutters his eyelashes and giggles

(*To both*) Now! Let's see what you be made of!
Captain } (*together, as themselves*) What!
Mate
Black Hook You be 'ere to dance! Let's see ye dance!

They dither

Dance, I say! (*He returns to his seat*)

The music starts and Captain and Mate perform a comic belly dance

18. Dance (Captain and Mate)

Peter enters L at the end of the dance and joins Jack at back

Vazar (*rising*) Now I will take my slaves and go. (*He moves* DR)
Black Hook Not yet! The celebrations ain't over! You must now drink wi'
me! (*To the Pirates*) Lads, bring in the grog!
Captain O Mighty Black Sheep! Let me fetch your groggy! (*He bows*)
Black Hook So be it! (*To the Pirates*) Go back to the ship. I shan't be
needin' 'ee anymore.
Jack } (*together*) Ay, Cap'n!
Peter

Jack and Peter exit C

Captain I go fetch your groggy-woggy!

The Captain bows and exits C

*The Mate hovers nervously, fiddling with his costume. He catches Black
Hook's eye. The Pirate gives Mate a huge wink. With a girlish toss of the
head, the Mate moves further away from dais*

Black Hook (*cooing and beckoning with his hook*) Yoo hoo, sweetykins.

The Mate giggles and acts coy

(*Cooing*) Sweetykins, come 'ere!

The Mate shakes his head and giggles

(*Bellowing*) Come 'ere!

*The Mate leaps in the air and runs on to the dais. Black Hook, leering,
presents his knee*

Sit down, my little desert flower.
Mate I'd rather thtand. I'm a growing girl.

Black Hook pulls the Mate on to his knee

Black Hook There! Ain't that comfy?

The Mate giggles

You be a trim little craft, ain't 'ee?

The Mate giggles

An' I bet you'm be pretty, ain't 'ee?

The Mate giggles

Let's 'ave a look behind this curtain! (*He goes to lift the Mate's yashmak with his hook*)

Mate (*pushing the hook away*) Naughty boy!

Black Hook (*cooing*) But I only want a little butchers!

Mate (*as himself*) Go thling yer hook!

Black Hook (*roaring*) What!

The Mate falls off Black Hook's knee and rolls off the dais

The Captain enters c, *carrying two goblets*

Captain Here is your wallop, O warty one!

Black Hook (*rising and taking a goblet*) Ar! Take t'other to me guest.

The Captain slinks to Vazar and hands him the goblet. Vazar does not drink. Black Hook empties his goblet in one gulp

Ha har! That be better! (*To Vazar*) Drink up, me bucko!

Vazar raises the goblet to his lips. Suddenly Black Hook starts coughing and spluttering. He drops his goblet and staggers about clutching his throat

Uur . . .! The drink . . .! Drugged! Ugh! Ahh!

He crashes to the ground and remains motionless. Vazar throws his goblet away. The Captain and Mate pull away their yashmaks

Vazar You two!

Captain Ay, 'tis us, you scurvy son of a shark! Mister Mate, get Sinbad and the others! I'll keep watch on this bilge rat!

The Mate runs out L

Vazar Ha! Ha! Ha! Do not think you have got the better of Vazar, the Mighty! You fools! Ha! Ha! Ha!

Sinbad, Monty and the Dame rush on L, *followed by the Mate*

Sinbad Cap'n! Am I glad to see you!

Dame (*to the audience, pointing at Black Hook*) Yipee! Someone's put his liver an' lights out!

Mate (*proudly*) That woth uth!

Dame My hero! (*She hugs him, then reacts to his outfit*) That colour doesn't suit you, dear!

Sinbad (*confronting Vazar*) So! We meet again, Vazar! But this time, you are in *my* power! Take us at once to the Valley of Skulls!

Vazar Never! You will never find it *or* the princess!
  (*Chanting*)   O Powers of Evil! O Powers Profane,
                        Transport me now to my secret domain!
  Ha! Ha! Ha!

There is a blinding flash and a Black-out

Vazar exits

The Lights return to normal

Captain By thunder! 'E's gorn an' gorn!
Dame What are we goin' to do, Sinny?
Sinbad We've got to search every part of this island until we find the Valley of Skulls!
Dame (*to the audience*) I was afraid 'e was goin' to say that!
Sinbad Come on!

  Led by Sinbad, they run out C. *Monty, the last to go, gives Black Hook a kick and scampers out after the others*

The Lights fade to Black-out

SCENE 5

Above the Valley of Skulls   ˅ ⊂ ⊂

The tabs or frontcloth as used in Act I, Scene 2

Vazar enters DR

Vazar Ha! Ha! Ha! I got away from those fools very easily! I suppose Sinbad is now searching for my Valley of Skulls! (*He looks over the edge of the stage*) Well, he's not going to find it, is he?

"Oh yes he is!", "Oh no he's not!" routine with the audience

  Ha! Even if he does—how is he going to get down to the princess? Only I, Vazar the Mighty, know the secret way into the valley. Ha! Ha! Ha! I am going now.

Audience: "Good"

  But I shall return and wreak havoc on you (*local*) morons!

  Shaking his fist, Vazar exits DL, *amid boos and hisses*

  The Captain, Mate and Dame enter DR. *She lags behind, footsore and weary. The Captain and Mate are back in their Arab robes*

Dame Oh, 'ang about! I can't keep up! All this flippin' walkin' an' climbin'.
Captain You've got to keep goin', Mother Sinbad! We've got to find the Valley of Skulls afore it gets dark.
Dame I can't go another step! All this sand an' heat! It makes me feel like Beau Geste!

Mate You look more like bow legth! (*He does his crazy laugh*)

Dame (*grabbing him and getting very dramatic*) I can't go on! I can't go on! The heat! *The heat!* Water! I must have water! (*She collapses against him*)

Mate (*shaking her and spitting in her face*) Thop it! You thilly thauthage! Thop it, I thay, thop it!

Dame (*basking in the spray*) Oo! Loverly, spray it again, Sam!

Captain Belay! Let's be gettin' on wi' the search!

Dame Oh, Captain, give me your arm for support. (*She takes his arm and cuddles close. In a deep sexy voice*) Now, I can go a little further!

Captain (*pushing her away*) You've gone far enough!!

Mate Hey, Cap'n! Look! (*Pointing over the edge of the stage*) Down there! It'th a valley!

Captain (*looking*) Shiver me timbers! That be it! The Valley of Skulls!

Mate (*looking and going dizzy*) Oh! How are we goin' to get down there?

Captain 'Tis impossible from 'ere. There must be another way down. Come on, Mister Mate, we'll go an' look! (*To the Dame*) You bide 'ere an' wait fer Sinbad.

The Captain and Mate run out L

Dame (*calling after them*) Don't leave me! It's spooky 'ere! (*To the audience, scared*) Oo! This place gives me the willies! (*She jumps with fright*) Ah! If you see anyone or (*she gulps*) any*thing*, give us a shout!

Barracuda creeps on R, *and moves behind the Dame*

Audience: "Behind you" etc. Comic business, then the Dame comes face to face with the Witch

Ahh! It's Jaws' Granny!!

Barracuda   Listen to me, you thing bizarre,
                      I've come to help my friend Vazar!
                      I have no magic power on land,
                      But still I'll give him a helping hand!

(*She advances on the Dame*)
                      You'll soon be dead, all cold and stiff,
                      For I'm going to push you over this cliff!

She pounces on the Dame and drags her to the front edge of the stage. They struggle C

Dame (*yelling*) Help! Sinbad! Save me! Help! Oooo!

Sinbad runs on DR. *The Captain and Mate run on* DL

Together, Sinbad and the Captain pull Barracuda away from the Dame and drag her R. *The Dame is teetering on the edge of the stage and the Mate pulls her back in the nick of time*

(*Clinging to the Mate*) Ooh! I saw the whole of me life flash before me! All twenty-one years of it!

Sinbad Are you all right, Mum?

Dame I think so, Sinny. No thanks to old nightmare Nellie over there!

Sinbad (*confronting Barracuda*) So! Are you here to put another curse on me?

Barracuda (*snarling and trying to pull away from the Captain*) Grrrr!

Dame Don't let 'er frighten you, son. The old jelly-fish ain't got no magic powers on land. She told me so 'erself! And look—(*pointing over the edge of stage*)—we've found the valley!

Sinbad Great! What are we waiting for? Let's get down there at once!

Captain 'Tis no good, lad. We've looked for a way down, an' there ain't one!

Sinbad is crestfallen

Barracuda (*a gloating cackle*) Hee! Hee! Hee!
     You've had it, Sinbad! That's all too plain!
     You'll never see your princess again!
Dame   Oh, put a sock in it, you silly old moo!
     Or I'll give ya a touch of the old one-two!

(*She rolls up her sleeves*)

Sinbad But there *must* be a way down! Some hidden steps, or——

Barracuda reacts

Captain She knows summit! (*Shaking her*) Out with it, Witch! Be there steps?

Barracuda Hee! Hee! Hee!
     There are steps down to the valley floor,
     But other than that, I'll say no more!
(*She rocks with mocking laughter*) Ha! Ha! Ha!

Monty scampers on DL and goes to the Dame

On seeing the monkey, Barracuda's laughter is cut short and she gives a piercing scream. She hides behind the Captain shaking with fear

     Ah! Keep it away, the horrible thing!
     Don't let it come near me, bad luck it will bring!
     I loathe all creatures who are covered in *that*!
     All cats, dogs and rabbits, and even the rat!
     I live in dread of the stuff that they wear,
     You see—*I'm allergic to animal hair!*

Sinbad So, Barracuda, we know your weakness. Now perhaps you will tell us where the steps are! Cap'n, hold her steady!

The Captain pulls the Witch from behind him. She squirms and struggles

     Mum, bring Monty over here!

Dame (*cackling à la Barracuda*) Hee! Hee! Hee! With pleasure! (*She takes Monty by the paw*) This way, you little *hairy* horror! Come and scare the scales off her! Hee! Hee! Hee!

She leads Monty over to Barracuda. The Witch shrinks back in horror and struggles to get free. Monty now realizes what he has to do, and waves his paw in front of Barracuda's face

Barracuda (*squirming*) Aww! Ugh! *No! No!*
Sinbad Where are the steps?

Barracuda shakes her head

Again, Monty!

Monty repeats the business

Where are the steps?
Barracuda (*giving in at last*)
　　　　　　　　　All right! All right! You win the day!
　　　　　　　　　I'll tell you all, just take it away!
Sinbad That's enough, Monty, old son!

Monty grunts with disappointment and moves away

(*To Barracuda*) Now, tell us! Where are the steps?
Barracuda (*pointing towards* L)
　　　　　　　　　Go to left, and you will find,
　　　　　　　　　A mighty boulder, the steps are behind!
　　　　　　　　　Some magic words you have to say,
　　　　　　　　　To make the boulder roll away!
Sinbad What are they?
Barracuda　　　Vazar will not be pleased with me!
　　　　　　　　　The magic words are: open sesame!
Dame (*to the audience*) As if you didn't know!

Monty rushes at Barracuda, gibbering and waving his paws

　Barracuda screams and runs out DR

Sinbad (*pointing off* L) Look! That must be the boulder!

All look

All we've got to do is say the magic words! After three! One! Two! Three!
All Open sesame!

They look. Nothing happens

Sinbad It didn't even tremble!
Dame We weren't loud enough, Sinny. Let's get everyone to holler! (*To the audience*) Come on, folks! Let's take the roof off! One! Two! Three!
Audience ⎱
All 　　　⎰ (*together*) Open sesame!

There is a blinding flash from off L, *loud rumbling noises are heard as the boulder rolls away*

Sinbad Hurray! The boulder's gone! (*To the audience*) Thanks, shipmates! (*To the others*) Come on! Let's go and rescue my princess!

Sinbad exits L

To suitable music, the others cheer and follow Sinbad off

The Lights fade to Black-out

SCENE 6

The Valley of Skulls

An eerie, gruesome-looking place. Prominent on each side are massive rocks shaped like human skulls. R, *the mouth of a skull forms the entrance to a dark cave. A groundrow of smaller skulls runs across the back. The backcloth shows the rest of the valley vanishing into the distance. Dim, weird lighting and ground mist*

If possible, the Lights change to UV *lighting as, to suitable music, the Skeleton Dancers leap on from all directions and go into their strange, spooky dance*

19. Dance (Skeleton Dancers)

After the dance, the Skeleton Dancers exit

The Lights become brighter

A timid group of Valley Dwellers, adults, and children, creep on L. *When they get* C, *Vazar enters* R, *dragging Yasmin behind him*

Vazar Ha! Ha! Ha! (*To the Dwellers*) Out of my way, you cringing curs! You worthless worms! (*He grabs one of the children and hurls her to the ground*)

Yasmin (*pulling free and going to the child's aid*) You cruel fiend! How dare you treat these poor people in this barbarous fashion!

Vazar I'll treat them any way I choose! They are my prisoners!

Yasmin Set them free at once! You have no right to keep them in this foul place. Set them free! I command it!

Vazar (*sneering*) *You* command it! Who are you to command me! This is *my* domain! You have no royal power here, my haughty one! These dogs will remain under my tender care! (*He cuffs one of the Dwellers*)

Yasmin You are nothing but a twisted, evil, ugly, nasty, vicious brute!

Vazar (*with a mocking bow*) Oh, Princess, you are too kind.

Yasmin charges at him with her fists flying. He grabs her by the wrists

Naughty! Naughty! This is no way to treat your lord and master! Listen, foolish girl. Show me some affection or I shall be forced to *make* you love me! My torture chamber can be very persuasive.

Yasmin (*pulling free*) Do what you will, Viper! I shall never love you! (*Facing front*) My heart belongs to another.

Vazar (*sneering*) Sinbad the Sailor, eh?

Yasmin (*facing him*) Yes!

Vazar Ha! Ha! I have outsmarted that young pup! He will never find you!
Forget all about him, and content yourself with me, my little pearl! (*He
moves towards her*)

Yasmin Touch me, and I will claw your evil eyes out!

Vazar (*backing off, knowing she means it*) I will leave you now . . .

Yasmin Allah be praised!

Vazar But I shall return shortly and I hope to find you in a friendlier mood!
If not, a visit to my torture chamber will help you to change your mind!
Ha! Ha! Ha!

Vazar sweeps off R

Yasmin O Allah! Guide Sinbad here to me. I feel in my heart that he is
somewhere near. Help him to save me from this vile monster.

Male Dweller Princess, do you really think your Sinbad is near?

Yasmin Yes, I do.

Female Dweller He must love you very much to risk his life against Vazar.

Yasmin Yes, and I love him. (*She sings*)

20. Song (Yasmin and Dwellers)

Male Dweller Do you think Sinbad would help us to escape, Princess?

Yasmin I promise you he will.

Dame (*off, from the cave*) Oy! Stop pushin'. Look out! Ahhh! Oooh!

*The Dame rolls out of the cave and lands in an undignified heap at Yasmin's
feet*

(*Sitting up*) Crikey! What a trip! (*She rubs her head*) Cor! I bet I've give
meself percussion. (*She staggers to her feet*)

Yasmin It's Mrs Sinbad!

Dame (*looking around*) Where . . . Oh! That's me! Yes, Semolina Sinbad at
your service! Hello, yer Royal Doulton! How ya diddlin'?

Yasmin (*eagerly*) Is . . . Has . . . Where's . . .?

Dame Now don't get yer royal knicks in a knot! Sailor boy's on his way!

Sinbad (*off, from the cave*) Ahoy there!

Sinbad runs from the cave, followed by Captain, Mate and Monty

(*Running straight to Yasmin and embracing her*) Yasmin!

Yasmin Sinbad!

Sinbad Oh, Yasmin!

Yasmin Oh, Sinbad!

Dame (*hugging Captain*) Oh, Captain!

Captain (*pushing her away*) Oh, push off!

Yasmin How did you find your way into the valley?

Sinbad By those steps in the cave. Surely you must have seen them.

Yasmin Yes, but the way out is blocked by a mighty stone.

Sinbad It's not anymore! Once up those steps and you're free.

Yasmin Sinbad. I gave my promise to these poor people that you would
help them to escape from Vazar.

Sinbad And I shall! Come, what are we waiting for!

Led by Sinbad, they all move towards the cave. There is a blinding flash and a great clap of thunder

With fiendish yells, the Skeleton Dancers leap on from the cave

The others retreat L

Vazar enters from the cave

Vazar Ha! Ha! Ha!

Dame Oh, no! It's the Black Adder again!

Vazar (*moving* C) So! You have managed to find your way into my secret valley! You are much cleverer than I thought, Sinbad the Sailor!

Sinbad What are you going to do?

Vazar Do? Well, as you were all so eager to get down here, I'm going to let you stay—*forever*! Those steps are your only way out! Take a good look at them, for they won't be there much longer!

Vazar moves to the cave and the lighting grows dark and sinister

> To those stone steps you can say your goodbyes!
> Now watch them vanish before your very eyes!
> (*He makes a magic pass at the cave*) Kalakazoom!

There is a flash inside the cave and a great stone rolls over, blocking the entrance. The lighting returns to normal

Ha! Ha! Ha! You fools! You are no match for Vazar, the Mighty! You're trapped! You will remain here until you grow old and *die*! All except *you*, Sinbad! You are not to suffer a life sentence! Very shortly you will be executed!

All react

Ha! Ha! I am going to feed you to—the roc! Ha! Ha! Ha!

Vazar sweeps out DR, *followed by the cackling Skeleton Dancers*

Dame 'E's bonkers! How is 'e goin' to feed you to a stick o' Blackpool (*or local*) rock!

Sinbad (*sadly*) It's not that sort of rock, Mum. Is it, Cap'n?

Captain (*with a sigh*) Nay, lad.

Sinbad (*putting his arms around the Dame and Yasmin*) Mum—darling—I don't know how to tell you this, but ... the roc is a ... a giant bird!

Dame (*laughing*) Pull the other one!

Captain 'Tis true! It flew over our ship once and its great wings blotted out the sky!

Dame Pah! You're havin' me on!

Dweller They speak the truth. The roc is a giant bird! We have seen it many times!

Dame Well, I don't believe it! (*To the audience*) Do you? Giant birds indeed! What a load of old rubbish! (*Ad lib until "roc" noises are heard*)

On the offstage microphone, the squawking of the "roc" is heard in the distance, as if above the audience

Captain 'Ark! What be that noise?

All listen. The squawking gets louder. Excitedly, Monty runs to the front of the stage and points out

Monty (*jumping up and down*) Oo! Oo! Oo!

All rush forward and look out. The squawking is now much louder and is accompanied by the flapping sound of gigantic wings

Dwellers It's the roc!

The noises get louder as the "roc" appears to be flying nearer to the stage

Sinbad It's heading straight at us!

All move back

Down!

All fall flat on the ground. The noises are now deafening and the lighting dims almost to black-out as the Giant Bird appears to fly right over the stage. Gradually, the lighting returns to normal and the noises fade away. All get to their feet, shaken. If possible, a giant feather floats down from above

Monty spots something off L, *and scampers out*

Dame (*optional: picking up the feather, to the audience*) Thank goodness, that's *all* it dropped! Yuck! (*She throws the feather off*)

Sinbad *Now*, do you believe us, Mum?

Dame Coo! What a whopper! Imagine tryin' to stuff that at Christmas! You'd need a flippin' bulldozer! (*Suddenly struck by the horror of it*) Ooh! Sinny! 'E's goin' to feed you to that ugly great budgie!

Monty enters L, *carrying an ornate casket*

Yasmin Oh, Sinbad, what are we going to do?

Sinbad I wish I knew! If only we——

Monty (*holding out the casket to Sinbad*) Oo! Oo!

Sinbad Hello! What have you got there, Monty? (*He takes the casket*) Where did you find this?

Monty (*pointing off* L) Oo! Oo!

Sinbad It must belong to Vazar. Let's see what's inside. (*He opens the casket and pulls out sparkling jewels, strings of pearls etc.*)

Dame It must be the old nasty's piggy-bank!

Sinbad (*to Yasmin*) With all this wealth your father could never object to me as a son-in-law! (*He sighs and replaces the treasure*) But I must put that thought out of my head! (*He gives the casket to the Dame*) I'm going to be bird's seed at any moment!

Yasmin (*in tears*) Oh, my poor Sinbad!

They turn away, comforting each other. The Dame and Monty move down and she opens the casket. She roots around and extracts a ring

Dame (*holding it up in disgust*) Lumme! How did *this* get in 'ere! A tatty old curtain ring! It's all . . . Hey! There's some written writin' on it! (*She peers* *at the ring*) Made in Hong Kong! Wait! There's somethin' else! (*Spelling out*) M.A.G.I.C. (*To the audience*) What's that mean? M.A.G.I.C.?

Audience: "Magic"

Go on with ya! You think this is a magic ring?

Audience: "Yes"

You lot are potty! There's no such thing as magic rings! This is just a dirty old bit o' brass! Look at the muck on it! (*She rubs it against her sleeve*)

There is a flash DL, *and a small green Genie appears, standing with arms folded*

All see the Genie, except the Dame who is looking at the ring. Monty pulls at her skirts

(*To Monty*) Don't do that, you little monkey! (*Seeing the Genie and jumping with fright*) Ahhh! It's the Jolly Green Giant!

Genie I am the Genie of the Magic Ring! (*Bowing*) You summoned me? I am yours to command! (*He bows*)

Dame (*to the audience*) Well! Chase me round the minaret! You were right! (*To the Genie*) Nice to meet you, Jean. (*To Sinbad*) What shall I do, Sinny?

Sinbad Ask him how many wishes you're granted.

Dame Oh, yeah! (*To the Genie*) How many wishes do I get, O Genie with the light brown ale?

Genie You are granted *one* wish, and *one* wish only. (*He bows*)

Dame Only *one*! 'Ow come I don't get three like Aladdin an' the rest o' them?

Genie I'm only a *small* Genie. What is your wish?

Dame Well, we don't want any cash, 'cos we've got this box o' sparklers! Now, I would like——

Sinbad Mum! Use your wish to get us away from here!

Dame Oh, yes! Silly me! Oh, this'll be one in the eye for Vazar! (*To the Genie*) I wish——

Genie One moment! Did you say Vazar?

Dame Yes.

Genie Vazar the Magician?

Dame That's the stinker.

Genie Many years ago he imprisoned me in that ring. He alone can release me from its power. If I had the chance, I could regain my freedom and put an end to his villainy at the same time.

Sinbad Vazar is certainly no friend of ours. Can we help?

Genie Yes. It will be necessary for you to give me the ring.

Dame 'Ang about!

Genie Let me explain. After granting a wish I automatically return to the ring. But if I am wearing it myself, that is impossible. I would then be able to meet Vazar face to face, bring about his downfall and regain my freedom.

Dame (*to the audience*) As clear as mud!

Sinbad Mum, give him the ring.

Genie Fear not! I shall still carry out your wish.
Dame Mind you do!

She gives the ring to the Genie who puts it on his finger

Genie (*bowing*) A thousand thanks to you! What is your wish?
Dame I wish we were all back in dear old Baghdad.
Genie Your wish is my command! (*He bows*)
Dame (*to the audience*) I just knew 'e was goin' to say that!
Genie All stand together, please.

All form a group upstage

Yasmin We hope you get your freedom, Genie.
Captain An' scuttle that swab Vazar!
Genie Please prepare yourselves.
Dame Fasten yer seatbelts, folks! We're about to have lift off! (*She clings to Captain*)

The Genie moves down C, and turns upstage with outstretched arms. Magical music

Genie   Away you go, over mountains and sea!
                           Return to Old Baghdad in time for tea!
         Kalakazoom!

There is a flash followed by a Black-out. The music continues

SCENE 7

Above the Valley of Skulls

The tabs or the frontcloth as used in Act II, Scenes 1 and 5

The Genie still stands as in the previous scene, facing upstage with his arms outstretched. The music fades out

Genie (*turning to the audience*) They will soon be back home in Baghdad. Now, I have to deal with Vazar!
Vazar (*off R*) Ha! Ha! Ha!

The Genie exits DL. Vazar enters DR

Ha! Ha! Ha! Very soon now Sinbad the Sailor will be bird's nest soup! (*He crosses to exit DL*)

Barracuda rushes on DR

Barracuda   Vazar! Vazar! The news is real chronic!
                 When you hear it you'll need a stiff gin and tonic!
                 Sinbad has slipped through your grasp again!
                 His luck is enough to drive you insane!

Vazar	Escaped again! Curse upon curse!
	Tell me how? I must know the worst!
Barracuda	I saw them all flying way up in the blue!
	The whole pack of fools and that monkey thing too!
Vazar	To where are they flying? Tell me their route!
	And on my magic carpet I'll give hot pursuit!
	On your flying doormat, you'd never compare!
Barracuda	They're faster than Concorde, of that I will swear!
	They are heading for Baghdad, of that I've no doubt,
	Let's face it, old son, you've had it! You're out!
Vazar	I will never give up! I must have my due!
	I'll get even with Sinbad, if it's the last thing I'll do.
Barracuda	I'll help you destroy the meddlesome brat!
	He cheated me twice, don't forget that!
Both	Together we'll get him, our forces we'll pool!
	With our magic powers we'll soon kill the fool!
Barracuda	I'll return to the sea and raise a great wave!
	It will cover all Baghdad, no-one will I save!
Vazar	Kill all if you like but leave Sinbad for me!
	I want him to die in slow agony!
Both (*to the audience*)	
	To Sinbad the Sailor you can all bid Adieu!
	Let us away! There is killing to do!
Ha! Ha! Ha!	

With menacing attitudes they creep towards the exit DR

The Genie leaps out in front of them

Genie (*making magic passes at them*) Kalakazoom!

Vazar and Barracuda are frozen in their menacing attitudes

(*To the audience*) What a lovely pair of garden gnomes they'd make! I bet they'd soon frighten off next-door's moggy! What shall I do with them?

The audience shout their bloodthirsty suggestions

No. Too messy. What's the best thing that can happen to a nasty? Why, turn him into a goody of course. And that's what I'm going to do with this pair. (*He moves away from them and raises his arms*)
     The powers of goodness I now invoke,
     Transform these nasties into nice, decent folk!
Kalakazoom! (*He claps his hands*)

Vazar and Barracuda come back to life, but with a great difference! They drop their menacing attitudes, put their hands together and smile angelically

Vazar	⎱ (*together, singing sweetly*)	"All things bright and beautiful,
Barracuda	⎰	all creatures great and small."

Genie It worked! Now to get my freedom. (*To Vazar*) Excuse me.

Vazar (*now a very benign gentleman*) Yes? (*To the audience*) Oh, what a sweet little green person.

Genie Years ago you imprisoned me in this ring.

Vazar Did I? How naughty of me. I'm very, very sorry. Is there any way I can make amends?

Genie You can set me free by repeating these words: Genie, Genie, your freedom I bring, you are no longer the Slave of the Ring!

Vazar Very well! (*To the audience*) Isn't this exciting! (*To the Genie*)
              Genie, Genie, your freedom I bring,
              You are no longer the Slave of the Ring.

Genie Now for the test. If I still remain visible after removing the ring, it has worked. Here goes! (*He takes a deep breath and removes the ring from his finger. To Vazar*) Can—can you still see me?

Vazar Yes.

Genie (*to the audience*) Can you?

Audience: "Yes"

Hurray! It worked! I'm free! Free! Freee!

The Genie dances off DL

Barracuda (*now a sweet lady*) Oh, I'm so pleased for him. Such a dear, sweet little thing.

Vazar (*making eyes at her*) And he's not the only one!

Barracuda (*very coy*) Oh, sir!

Vazar (*taking her hand*) Come, my little water-lily! Let us trip the light fantastic together!

To suitable music, they perform a short, soppy dance

Hand in hand, they skip off, waving to the audience as they go

The Lights fade to a Black-out

SCENE 8

Before the wedding

Tabs or a frontcloth

The Dame and Monty bounce on, waving to the audience. The Dame wears a comic hat and smock that can be easily changed for the finale costume

Dame Hello, folks! Hi, kids! Well, that's yer lot! Everything's turned out fine, hasn't it, Monty? The baddies are now goodies, the genie's got his freedom, we're rich, the sultan's going to let Sinbad marry the beautiful princess and—this is the best bit of all—the captain is going to marry beautiful *me*!

Monty Oo! Oo! Oooo!

Dame (*to Monty*) What do you mean—'e's only after me money?

The Captain and Mate enter. They wear their naval costumes

Oh, there 'e is! (*She hugs the Captain*) Me financee! Let's get down to (*local travel agent*) an' book the honeymoon!

Captain There be summit I wants to do wi' 'ee first, Semolina—(*with a grimace*)—my love!

Dame Oo! What? Oh, he wants to whisper sweet nothin's.

He whispers in her ear

(*Shocked*) What now?

Captain Ar!

Dame Here?

Captain Ar!

Dame (*giving him a playful push*) Oh, you saucy old sea salt you! (*To the audience*) Guess what he wants to do? Oh, you rude lot! No, he wants you all to join us in a sing-song! Yah! You thought you'd got away with it, didn't ya?

Captain Mister Mate!

Mate Yeth, Cap'n!

The Mate runs off and returns, leading the Camel. It has a song sheet attached to its hump. It should be a well known song of the "What shall we do with the drunken sailor" variety

Captain 'Ere be (*camel's name*) wi' the words. (*To the audience*) Now, you all know this one, shipmates! (*To the pianist or conductor*) Music, Mr Christian!

21. Song (Dame, Captain, Mate and Audience)

They get the audience to sing along. Comic business with the Camel turning around and obscuring the words, etc. The Mate can do his crazy laugh

It ends with the Camel dancing off followed by the others, waving and shouting "Goodbye" "Ta! Ta!" to the audience

The Lights fade to Black-out. The gong sounds

Scene 9

Sinbad's wedding. Finale

A glittering "Arabian Nights" setting with an archway and steps at the back

The Chorus enter singing

22. Song (Reprise)

Finale walk-down. The last to enter is Sinbad and Yasmin

Sinbad Our tale of Sinbad has been told.

Yasmin We hope you liked it, both young and old.

Sultan 'Tis time to leave this Arabian night.

Dame (*hugging the Captain*)
        I'm now the Cap'n's Turkish Delight!
Barracuda
        We've given up our evil ways.
Vazar   Next week we star on *Songs of Praise*.
Black Hook
        A pirate no more, I'll sling me hook.
Mate   Don't lithen to him, he'th thill an old crook!

Genie   We hope the magic of tonight has cast its spell on *you*.
        And Monty now would like to say——

Monty   Oo! Oo! Oo! Oo! Oo! *Ooo!*

Captain   A safe voyage home, be ye tinker or tailor!

All   Good-night and God bless from Sinbad the Sailor!

Final chorus

CURTAIN

FURNITURE AND PROPERTY LIST

ACT I

SCENE 1

On stage: Baghdad backcloth
Harbour wall, rostrum and steps
Palace and steps
Stalls with carpets, pots, etc.

Off stage: Shopping bag. *In it:* sweets, "bouncing" egg in egg carton (**Dame**)
Large fake cabbage (**Stage Management**)
Scimitars (**Guards**)
Staff (**Vizier**)
Magic box. *In it:* carpet (**Hassan**)
Golden Hawk cut-out (**Stage Management**)
Large Ali-Baba basket (**Captain** and **Mate**)
Suitcase, hat-box, bird-cage (**Dame**)

Personal: **Dame**: handkerchief
Vazar: dagger (worn throughout)
Mate: toy parrot on shoulder

SCENE 2

On stage: Tabs or frontcloth

SCENE 3

On stage: Galley backcloth
Ship's mast, rigging and sails
Table. *On it:* check cloth, rolling pin, cooking utensils, cookery book, bowl of "dumplings"

SCENE 4

On stage: Sky backcloth
Bulwarks
Ship's mast, rigging and sails
Barrels, chests etc.
Fishing line on barrel

Off stage: Large telescope (**Captain**)
Sea charts (**Mate**)
Sea Serpent (**Stage Management**)
Pirate ship cut-out (**Stage Management**)
Cutlasses, pistols (**Pirates**)
Skull and Crossbone flag (**Pirate**)
Cutlasses (**Crew**)
Cutlasses for **Sinbad** and **Captain** (**Crew**)

Personal: **Sinbad:** slice of tart in pouch
Black Hook: hook, cutlass, pistols (worn throughout)

ACT II
SCENE 1

On stage: Tabs or frontcloth

SCENE 2

On stage: Desert backcloth
Wall with archway
Inn. *On it:* sign reading "Ye Olde Camel's Hump"
Rostrum. *On it:* sign reading "Super Slave Sale Today"

Off stage: Tankard (**Black Hook**)
Sweets for children in the audience (**Mate**)

Personal: **Vazar:** money bag

SCENE 3

On stage: Tabs or frontcloth

Off stage: Rope (**Sinbad**, **Dame**, **Monty**)

SCENE 4

On stage: Tent cut cloth or drapes
Dais with seat or divan

Off stage: 2 goblets (**Captain**)

SCENE 5

On stage: Tabs or frontcloth

SCENE 6

On stage: Valley backcloth
Skull rocks
Cave entrance R
Skull groundrow

Off stage: Giant feather (optional) (**Stage Management**)
Casket. *In it:* magic ring, jewels, pearls etc. (**Monty**)

SCENE 7

On stage: Tabs or frontcloth

SCENE 8

On stage: Tabs or frontcloth

Off stage: Song sheet (**Camel**) ·

SCENE 9

On stage: Archway and steps for walk-down

LIGHTING PLOT

Property fittings required: nil

Various interior and exterior settings

ACT I, SCENE 1

To open: General external lighting

Cue 1	**Sinbad:** "I think you know." *Change to romantic lighting*	(Page 9)
Cue 2	At the end of Song 6 *Revert to general external lighting*	(Page 9)
Cue 3	**Vazar:** "Up magic carpet and fly away!" *Dim lighting*	(Page 14)
Cue 4	**Vazar:** "Up and away! Ha! Ha! Ha!" *Flash.* *Black-out. When ready bring up external lighting*	(Page 14)
Cue 5	All wave and the ship sails off . *Fade to black-out*	(Page 17)

ACT 1, SCENE 2

To open: Eerie external lighting

Cue 6	**Vazar:** "Kazoom!" *Dim lighting, bring up spots on* **Vazar** *and* **Yasmin**	(Page 17)
Cue 7	**Vazar:** "To my secret lair!" *Snap out spot on* **Yasmin**. *When ready, revert to eerie external lighting and snap out spot on* **Vazar**	(Page 18)
Cue 8	**Vazar:** ". . . Witch of the Sea to help me." *Dim lighting, bring up spot on* **Vazar**	(Page 18)
Cue 9	**Vazar:** ". . . I am in need of thy help!" *Eerie green spot on* **Barracuda**	(Page 18)
Cue 10	**Barracuda:** "Hee! Hee! Hee!" *Snap out spot on* **Barracuda**	(Page 19)
Cue 11	**Vazar** exits *Fade to black-out*	(Page 19)

ACT I, SCENE 3

To open: General interior lighting

Cue 12	*The* **Mate** exits *Fade to black-out*	(Page 22)

ACT I, SCENE 4

To open: General external lighting

Cue 13	**Sinbad** starts to sing Song 10 *Gradual crossfade to spot on* **Sinbad**	(Page 25)
Cue 14	**Sinbad** falls asleep *Crossfade to "dream" lighting*	(Page 25)
Cue 15	**Yasmin** and the **Handmaidens** exit *Crossfade to general external lighting*	(Page 25)
Cue 16	All heave on the fishing line *Dim lighting, bring up weird flickering lights from the sea and eerie green spot on* **Sea Serpent**	(Page 25)
Cue 17	**Sea Serpent** sinks from sight *Revert to general external lighting*	(Page 26)

ACT II, SCENE 1

To open: Eerie external lighting

Cue 18	**Barracuda** enters *Eerie green spot on* **Barracuda**	(Page 30)
Cue 19	**Vazar** and **Barracuda** exit *Fade to black-out*	(Page 31)

ACT II, SCENE 2

To open: General external lighting

Cue 20	**Dame:** "Music! Lights! Action!" *Bring up follow spot on* **Dame**	(Page 34)
Cue 21	The **Dame** ends the dance and strikes a pose *Snap out follow spot on* **Dame**	(Page 34)
Cue 22	**Captain:** "Now, who be comin' up?" *Bring up house lights*	(Page 37)
Cue 23	When the children have returned to their seats *Fade house lights*	(Page 37)
Cue 24	At the end of Song 16 *Fade to black-out*	(Page 40)

ACT II, SCENE 3

To open: General external lighting

Cue 25	The **Mate** and **Belly Dancers** exit *Fade to black-out*	(Page 42)

ACT II, SCENE 4

To open: General interior lighting

Cue 26	**Vazar:** "Ha! Ha! Ha!" *Black-out. When ready, revert to general interior lighting*	(Page 47)
Cue 27	**Monty** scampers out *Fade to black-out*	(Page 47)

ACT II, Scene 5

To open: Eerie external lighting

Cue 28	**Sinbad** and the others exit *Fade to black-out*	(Page 51)

ACT II, Scene 6

To open: Dim weird lighting

Cue 29	The **Skeleton Dancers** leap on *Change to UV lighting (if possible)*	(Page 51)
Cue 30	The **Skeleton Dancers** exit *Cut UV effect and increase to general lighting*	(Page 51)
Cue 31	**Vazar** moves to the cave *Dim lighting*	(Page 53)
Cue 32	**Vazar:** "Kalakazoom!" Pause *Revert to general lighting*	(Page 53)
Cue 33	All fall flat on the ground *Reduce to an almost imperfect black-out, then gradually bring up to previous general lighting*	(Page 54)
Cue 34	The **Dame** rubs the ring *Bring up follow spot on* **Genie**	(Page 55)
Cue 35	**Genie:** "Kalakazoom!" *Black-out*	(Page 56)

ACT II, Scene 7

To open: Eerie external lighting with follow spot on **Genie**

Cue 36	The **Genie** exits *Snap out follow spot on* **Genie**	(Page 56)
Cue 37	The **Genie** leaps on DR *Bring up follow spot on* **Genie**	(Page 57)
Cue 38	The **Genie** exits. *Snap out follow spot on* **Genie**	(Page 58)
Cue 39	**Vazar** and **Barracuda** exit *Fade to black-out*	(Page 58)

ACT II, Scene 8

To open: General lighting

Cue 40	Everyone exits *Fade to black-out*	(Page 59)

ACT II, Scene 9

To open: Bright general lighting

No cues

EFFECTS PLOT

ACT I

Cue 1   The **Dame** exits DR   (Page 2)
Gong

Cue 2   **Vizier:** "... the Sultan of Baghdad!"   (Page 2)
Gong

Cue 3   **Sultan:** "Behold! The Princess Yasmin!"   (Page 2)
Gong

Cue 4   **2nd Man:** "... like *that* into his palace."   (Page 4)
Ship's bell UR

Cue 5   **Monty** exits DL   (Page 11)
Gong

Cue 6   **Sinbad:** "The Sultan is coming!"   (Page 12)
Gong

Cue 7   **Vizier:** "... the Princess Yasmin!"   (Page 12)
Gong

Cue 8   **Sultan:** "Vazar, the Mighty!"   (Page 12)
Flash

Cue 9   **Vazar:** "Up and away! Ha! Ha! Ha!"   (Page 14)
Flash, then weird sounds of flying carpet

Cue 10   **Dame Sinbad** exits DR   (Page 16)
Gong

Cue 11   **Vazar:** "Kazoom!"   (Page 17)
Flash

Cue 12   **Vazar:** "To my secret lair!"   (Page 18)
Flash

Cue 13   **Vazar:** "... I am in need of thy help!"   (Page 18)
Flash

Cue 14   **Barracuda:** "Hee! Hee! Hee!"   (Page 19)
Flash

Cue 15   **Sinbad** falls asleep   (Page 25)
Ground mist

Cue 16   All heave on the fishing line   (Page 25)
Flash, thunderclap, strange noises, sea mist

Cue 17   **Captain:** "Stand by to repel boarders!"   (Page 27)
Sea-battle noises